Buddhism

A Guide to the Fundamental Beliefs and Traditions of Buddhism and Present

(Insights From Buddhism to Cultivate Peace and Harmony)

Steven Phinney

Published By **Ryan Princeton**

Steven Phinney

All Rights Reserved

Buddhism: A Guide to the Fundamental Beliefs and Traditions of Buddhism and Present (Insights From Buddhism to Cultivate Peace and Harmony)

ISBN 978-1-7752619-5-7

No part of this guidebook shall be reproduced in any form without permission in writing from the publisher except in the case of brief quotations embodied in critical articles or reviews.

Legal & Disclaimer

The information contained in this book is not designed to replace or take the place of any form of medicine or professional medical advice. The information in this book has been provided for educational & entertainment purposes only.

The information contained in this book has been compiled from sources deemed reliable, and it is accurate to the best of the Author's knowledge; however, the Author cannot guarantee its accuracy and validity and cannot be held liable for any errors or omissions. Changes are periodically made to this book. You must consult your doctor or get professional medical advice before using any of the suggested remedies, techniques, or information in this book.

Upon using the information contained in this book, you agree to hold harmless the Author from and against any damages, costs, and expenses, including any legal fees potentially resulting from the application of any of the information provided by this guide. This disclaimer applies to any damages or injury caused by the use and application, whether directly or indirectly, of any advice or information presented, whether for breach of contract, tort, negligence, personal injury, criminal intent, or under any other cause of action.

You agree to accept all risks of using the information presented inside this book. You need to consult a professional medical practitioner in order to ensure you are both able and healthy enough to participate in this program.

Table Of Contents

Chapter 1: The Four Noble Truths 1

Chapter 2: The Noble Eight Fold Path 15

Chapter 3: The Five Hindrances 37

Chapter 4: Meditation And Mindfulness 59

Chapter 5: Karma And Rebirth 83

Chapter 6: The Three Schools Of Buddhism 97

Chapter 7: Origins Of Buddhism 108

Chapter 8: Requirements And Practices 123

Chapter 9: Beliefs And Philosophy 134

Chapter 10: Buddhism Within The Modern World 141

Chapter 11: Interfaith Dialogue And Buddhism 149

Chapter 12: Buddhism And Ethics 155

Chapter 13: Buddhism And Mindfulness 162

Chapter 14: Buddhism And The Path To Liberation.. 170

Chapter 15: Buddhist Practices And Rituals
.... 179

Chapter 1: The Four Noble Truths

In a global that is constantly changing, there exist positive truths, steadfast and unwavering. These truths, recognized and taught thru the Buddha, are referred to as the Four Noble Truths. They are not depending on the presence of a Buddha inside the worldwide; they exist universally, irrespective of time and area.

The Four Noble Truths:

Suffering exists (Dukkha).

Suffering has a reason (Samudaya).

Suffering can give up (Nirodha).

There is a route most important to the cessation of struggling (Magga).

These truths aren't to be taken as pessimistic or bad; as an opportunity, they offer a practical attitude of lifestyles as it's miles. The Buddha did not deny the life of pleasure and happiness. Instead, he identified the ones evaluations as fleeting. True happiness, constant with the Buddha, lies in understanding and transcending those brief evaluations of lifestyles.

They provide a framework for facts the stressful conditions we're going through in our lives - whether or now not it's strain at artwork, courting troubles, or fitness troubles. By facts the character of suffering and its motive, we're capable of paintings towards its cessation.

This quote fantastically encapsulates the essence of the Four Noble Truths. It reminds us of the inevitability of getting antique, illness, and loss of existence - the final varieties of struggling. It moreover points toward the course to the cessation of suffering: residing gently, loving deeply, and letting pass gracefully.

The Truth of Dukkha (Suffering)

"The handiest way out of struggling is through it." This quote isn't from some ancient

Buddhist textual content; it's from Carl Jung, one of the forefathers of cutting-edge psychology. Yet, it encapsulates an crucial reality about Buddhism's first Noble Truth: The reality of Dukkha, or struggling.

Dukkha is regularly translated as suffering, however it encompasses a lot more. It represents the unsatisfactoriness, discontent, and present day unease that pervades our lives. Life, in its impermanent nature, is complete of moments of pride, pain, love, and loss. But under the floor, there resides an ever-gift undercurrent of dissatisfaction, longing for topics to be one-of-a-type than they may be. This is Dukkha.

Let me percentage a personal tale. Several years inside the past, I positioned myself in a interest that I had tirelessly pursued. I changed into earning a terrific profits, had a good characteristic, and become surrounded by way of way of fellow workers who regarded as much as me. Yet, each morning, I might awaken with a heavy feeling in my coronary heart. The artwork wasn't attractive, and I felt a constant feel of discontent. That became my first actual come upon with Dukkha.

The Three Fires (Poisons)

Buddhism teaches us that the foundation cause of Dukkha is the Three Fires, regularly referred to as the Three Poisons. They are Greed, Hatred, and Delusion.

Greed (yearning, desire, thirst):

Greed, in Buddhism, isn't just about trying extra money or possessions. It's approximately the ceaseless craving for extra - greater opinions, extra reputation, greater happiness. It's this consistent thirst that maintains us caught in a cycle of dissatisfaction. When I changed into in that immoderate-paying activity, I turn out to be constantly trying to find the subsequent vending, the following large challenge, the subsequent signal of fulfillment. Yet, each success most effective precipitated a short immoderate that brief dwindled, fundamental to more cravings.

Hatred (aversion, aggression):

Hatred, or aversion, is the opportunity side of the coin. It's approximately resisting what is, pushing away what we discover uncomfortable or ugly. It's our tendency to lash out in anger or retreat in fear at the same time as topics don't cross our manner. I found out I emerge as doing this as soon as I positioned myself continuously complaining approximately my process, feeling annoyed with my colleagues, and resisting the paintings I had to do.

Delusion (loss of records, confusion):

The very last hearth is fable, the foundation of the opposite . Delusion is our important lack of information approximately the way topics are. It's our faulty notion that we are able to find out lasting happiness in temporary subjects, our confusion approximately what definitely subjects in existence. In my case, I become underneath the fable that fulfillment and recognition should deliver me lasting happiness.

To triumph over the ones fires, we want to cultivate their antidotes: generosity for greed, loving-kindness for hatred, and information for myth. This is the coronary coronary heart of the Buddhist route.

To illustrate, permit's remember this section from a famous story:

"Two priests have been on a pilgrimage. They came to a river in which they met a lovely younger lady not capable of cross. The elder monk carried her in the course of, no matter the fact that priests have been forbidden to touch ladies. Later, the younger monk asked, 'Why did you do this?' The elder monk answered, 'I left the girl on the river. Are you still sporting her?'"

This story especially illustrates how our minds, clouded via the use of delusions, regularly maintain immediately to topics prolonged after their relevance has handed, inflicting useless struggling.

Samudaya: The Truth of the Cause of Dukkha (Suffering) - Desire

"A guy is however the made from his thoughts. What he thinks, he will become." - Mahatma Gandhi. The essence of this quote is a first rate segue into the second one Noble Truth of Buddhism - Samudaya, the begin of Dukkha or suffering, it is essentially rooted in preference.

Picture this. You're status in the front of a bakery, the aroma of freshly baked bread wafting out. Suddenly, you're overwhelmed thru a robust preference for a pastry. You weren't hungry earlier than, but now you revel in a gnawing on your belly. You purchase the pastry and for a 2d, you're happy. But fast after, the satisfaction wanes, and you're left searching a few aspect else. This cycle of choice and temporary delight is a center factor of human existence.

Buddhism teaches us that the reason of our suffering is Tanha, frequently translated as 'thirst', 'choice', or 'yearning'. It's the craving for sensual pleasures, for existence and non-lifestyles, for recognition, for love, for the entirety that we accept as true with will make us satisfied. We are driven via a steady need for added - more meals, more money, extra success, extra validation. We get trapped in an infinite cycle of preference and temporary pride, determined via the usage of the use of extra choice. It's like being on a treadmill, usually taking walks but in no manner carrying out our destination due to the reality the give up line maintains moving.

But permit's pause for a second. Is desire inherently terrible? After all, isn't it desire that drives us to beautify, to create, to gain? Here's wherein it gets exciting. Buddhism doesn't educate that desire in itself is terrible. Instead, it's our attachment to those goals that reason struggling. It's on the equal time as we emerge as so entangled in our needs that we lose sight of the bigger photograph and get caught up in a harmful cycle of craving and dissatisfaction.

Let's bypass returned to the bakery example. It's not incorrect to desire the pastry and revel in it. The trouble arises while we turn out to be so fixated at the pastry, so related to the fast pleasure it gives, that we go through as a stop result. Maybe we revel in guilty for indulging, or probable we're upset at the same time as the pastry doesn't flavor as accurate as we'd hoped. Our attachment to the very last consequences - to the idea of the pastry making us glad - is what motives struggling.

Nirodha: The Truth of the End of Dukkha (Suffering)

Mindfulness:

The cornerstone of the direction. To recognize is to be present, to take a look at with out judgment, and to be privy to your mind, emotions, and the area round you. It is to live within the second, now not misplaced within the beyond or disturbing approximately the destiny. A few years within the beyond, I became stuck up in a whirlwind of obligations. Mindfulness allowed me to step back, breathe, and recognize the beauty of the present second.

Discernment:

The artwork of data whether or not an movement may be skillful or unskilful. It's approximately selecting the proper direction at the same time as faced with crossroads. Once, I had to pick out among a excessive-paying technique that demanded lengthy hours and a process that paid lots less however provided extra time for personal increase and happiness. Discernment guided me to pick the latter.

Persistence:

The engine that powers your journey. It is the self-discipline to live on the course, in spite of the bounds you could stumble upon. It is set in no way giving up. Remember Thomas

Edison? He persisted thru a thousand failed attempts in advance than inventing the moderate bulb.

Rapture:

The pleasure that arises from strolling the direction, from seeing the quit result of your practice. It is the exhilaration of a runner nearing the give up line, the satisfaction of an artist out of place within the act of creation. Rapture is the reward to your persistence.

Serenity:

As you development to your course, you'll find out a experience of calm descending upon you. This is serenity, the peace that comes from knowing you're at the proper path. It's the tranquillity of a lake at sunrise, the quiet of a wooded location at night time.

Concentration:

The capability to awareness your mind, to direct your hobby in which you pick out out. Concentration is the lens that magnifies the moderate of mindfulness, illuminating the path earlier. It is the stillness in the eye of the typhoon.

Equanimity:

The final element of awakening is equanimity. It is the ability to stay calm and balanced, regardless of the conditions. It's the mountain that stays unmoved thru the typhoon. Equanimity isn't always indifference; it's a deep facts of the temporary nature of all topics.

These Seven Factors of Awakening are the keys to the give up of struggling. They are not sequential but interdependent and together supportive. Each trouble complements and is extra through the others. They are just like the strings of a guitar; while strummed collectively, they produce a concord that outcomes in the symphony of enlightenment.

Nirvana Demystified: An Enlightened Exploration

"Enlightenment is not approximately turning into divine. Instead, it's approximately turning into extra completely human..." - Lama Surya Das. With this powerful quote lighting our path, permit's embark on an highbrow journey. We're occurring a adventure some distance past the location of the mundane, in which we'll unfurl the mystic idea of Nirvana.

Before we prompt, permit me make a confession. This confession is about Nirvana, and the truth that it had me scratching my head for years. Like a jigsaw puzzle with a thousand tiny pieces, Nirvana seemed like a concept a long way too grand to apprehend. Until sooner or later, I had a revelation that allowed me to place the quantities collectively.

Nirvana. A phrase that's been thrown round, twisted, became, and commercialized with the aid of manner of famous way of life. A time period that's come to be as ubiquitous as a latte order at Starbucks. "I'll have a caramel macchiato and a element of Nirvana, please!" Funny, isn't it? Well, we're about to strip lower back the layers of false impression and delve into the actual essence of Nirvana. Buckle up, because of the fact that is going to be one enlightening adventure!

Nirvana, often appeared as a miles off, airy motive, an impossible kingdom of herbal bliss, can appear to be a mountain too steep to climb. But what if I informed you the mountain isn't as excessive as you watched? What if, actually what if, Nirvana have become heaps a great deal much less about accomplishing the summit and additional about appreciating the climb?

Chapter 2: The Noble Eight Fold Path

"Peace comes from inside Do not are trying to find it without. " This beautiful aphorism from Gautama Buddha serves as a moderate reminder that the direction to tranquility and enlightenment starts offevolved with our inner selves. This introspective adventure is guided via the Eightfold Path, a chain of standards that Buddha taught because the Middle Way to attain Nirvana.

The Eightfold Path consists of those factors:

Right View:

Understanding the Four Noble Truths and the man or woman of fact.

Right Thought:

Cultivating selfless, loving, and compassionate mind.

Right Speech:

Speaking actually, kindly, and constructively.

Right Action:

Acting ethically and refraining from risky behaviors.

Right Livelihood:

Choosing a profession that aligns with moral mind.

Right Effort:

Consistently striving to beautify oneself and cultivate superb thoughts-states.

Right Mindfulness:

Being without a doubt gift and aware of one's thoughts, feelings, and actions.

Right Concentration:

Developing the intellectual reputation critical for deep meditation.

The time period 'Right' on this context, as Buddha intended, is in the route of our modern-day expertise of 'appropriate' or 'realistic'. These aren't dogmatic hints however guides to conduct that results in happiness and faraway from struggling.

In essence, the Eightfold Path is ready stability. It steers us far from the extremes of self-indulgence and self-mortification, guiding us closer to a slight, balanced route that cultivates internal peace and information. This route transcends the simplistic notions of proper and wrong, as an alternative guiding us in the direction of facts the outcomes of our moves on ourselves and others.

The Three Divisions of the Path

"A journey of 1 thousand miles starts with a single step," stated Lao Tzu, an historic Chinese logician. This facts applies perfectly to the journey through Buddhism. In our exploration, we begin with the Three Divisions of the Path: Wisdom, Morality, and Meditation.

Wisdom, called 'Prajna' in Sanskrit, is the primary department we encounter on this route. It's just like the compass of our journey, directing our thoughts and actions. Right View and Right Thought, the primary factors of the Noble Eightfold Path, fall underneath Wisdom. Imagine yourself because of the reality the Beatles' George Harrison, who have grow to be deeply inspired with the useful resource of Eastern philosophy. As he sang in 'Within You Without You', he grasped the essence of Right View and Right Thought - seeing and know-how the interconnectedness of all subjects and releasing the mind of greed, hate, and myth.

The second branch, Morality or 'Sila', is the embodiment of our information inside the physical global. It's the code of ethics guiding our interactions with others and the arena round us. Right Speech, Right Action, and Right Livelihood represent this department. Picture yourself as His Holiness the Dalai Lama, who personifies those ideas in his every day existence. He makes use of phrases to inspire, uplift, and impart awareness (Right Speech). His movements are within the provider of others and within the route of the renovation of peace (Right Action), and he consciously chooses a existence that aligns collectively along along with his spiritual ideals (Right Livelihood).

The 1/3 department, Meditation or 'Samadhi', is the tool that sharpens our mind and heightens our focus. This branch consists of Right Effort, Right Mindfulness, and Right Concentration.

Visualize those 3 divisions because the spokes of a wheel - the Dharma Wheel. This symbolic wheel is not truly any wheel. It's an logo of Buddhist dharma, the schooling of Buddha that bring about enlightenment. Each of its 8 spokes represents a step on the Noble Eightfold Path. The hub stands for ethical vicinity which supports the complete direction, and the rim, which holds the spokes, signifies mindfulness and consciousness that maintain us on the right tune.

The Dharma Wheel

The Dharma Wheel, also called the Dharmachakra, is a symbol that represents

Buddhism and Buddhist teachings. The wheel consists of 3 predominant factors:

Hub: Represents the Three Jewels of Buddhism, which is probably the Buddha (the enlightened one), Dharma (the classes), and Sangha (the network of believers).

Spokes: These represent the Eightfold Path, which is probably the practices that result in enlightenment. These include Right View, Right Intention, Right Speech, Right Action, Right Livelihood, Right Effort, Right Mindfulness, and Right Concentration.

Rim: This represents the attention that holds the whole thing collectively.

The beauty of this route lies in its stability - the Middle Way. It's neither an ascetic existence of self-denial nor a hedonistic pursuit of sensory pleasures. It's a course that avoids those extremes and as an possibility, encourages a life of moderation and mindfulness. This Middle Way leads in the end to Nirvana, the country of last peace and liberation from struggling.

Following this route could likely revel in daunting, like a adventure of 1 thousand miles. But hold in thoughts Lao Tzu's understanding: it all starts offevolved with a unmarried step. Your step. So, are you ready to embark in this transformative adventure to Wisdom, Understanding, Loving Kindness, Compassion, Calm, and Peace.

THE THREE JEWELS

One of the foundational steps inside the direction of such transformation is knowing and taking refuge inside the Three Jewels, particularly the Buddha, Dharma, and Sangha. These are often called the Three Treasures of Buddhism and characteristic guiding lighting fixtures for your non secular adventure. Let's delve a piece deeper into those treasured treasures.

The Yellow Jewel - The Buddha

The Buddha shows the enlightened one, the teacher who completed remaining knowledge and shared his information with the place. It's not absolutely the historical Buddha, Siddhartha Gautama, that we speak over with proper here, but the Buddha nature inherent in each one humans. It's the capability for attention and compassion that everyone private. Taking safe haven within the Buddha manner spotting and nurturing this functionality.

To bring this concept to lifestyles, endure in thoughts the tale of American actor Keanu Reeves. Despite going thru severa personal tragedies, he positioned solace and energy in Buddhism. His reverence for the Buddha helped him recognize his inner functionality for resilience and compassion, in the long run permitting him to influence a lifestyles of kindness and generosity. He's a living example of the Buddha nature inner surely each person.

The Blue Jewel - The Dharma

The Dharma represents the lessons of the Buddha, the truths he located out in the path of his enlightenment. It is the path that ends in statistics and liberation from struggling. When you are taking secure haven inside the Dharma, making a decision to following those teachings, to important a life of mindfulness and compassion, to know-how the interconnectedness of all beings.

Think of Dharma as a compass guiding you thru the turbulent sea of existence. It's the navigation machine imparting you with directions for your vacation spot - a state of peace, expertise, and liberation.

The Red Jewel - The Sangha

The Sangha embodies the network of fellow practitioners, the ones walking alongside you on the direction of the Dharma. It is the fellowship of seekers, the guide system that facilitates you stay the direction. When you take safe haven within the Sangha, you emerge as a part of this spiritual community, lending and receiving useful resource, sharing recollections and learnings.

Consider the instance of famend singer Tina Turner. Despite her disturbing past, she placed strength within the exercise of Buddhism, in particular inside her Sangha. Her non secular community provided her with the crucial guide and encouragement to persevere through her struggles. It's via this communal help that people regularly discover the electricity to keep their journey.

Taking secure haven in the Three Jewels is a critical thing of Buddhism. It's about spotting and nurturing your inherent ability for interest and compassion (Buddha), committing to a course that ends in statistics and liberation (Dharma), and becoming a part of a supportive non secular network (Sangha). It's thru this act of taking refuge that you begin your adventure closer to transformation, in the direction of identifying unsurpassed freedom.

Let's assessment the Three Jewels all over again:

1. The Buddha (Yellow Jewel): Recognizing and nurturing your inherent functionality for understanding and compassion, including Keanu Reeves.

2. The Dharma (Blue Jewel): Committing to a path that ends in expertise and liberation, like a compass guiding via existence.

three. The Sangha (Red Jewel): Becoming a part of a supportive religious community, collectively with Tina Turner.

In your journey inside the path of statistics Buddhism and integrating its thoughts into your life, preserve in thoughts the ones 3 jewels. They function beacons, guiding you in the direction of a existence of knowledge, loving-kindness, compassion, calm, and peace.

THE FIVE PRECEPTS: THE MORAL CODE

" In order to maintain a brilliant movement, we need to boom proper right right here a nice vision ," said the Dalai Lama, an inspiring parent who has been a beacon of desire for masses. This quote serves as a reminder that the muse of our moves lies within the ethical code that we test. In Buddhism, this code is encapsulated with the resource of the Five Precepts, which form an essential part of the Noble Eightfold Path.

The Five Precepts, also called The Five Virtues, offer a framework for moral behavior within the international. These guiding ideas are vital due to the fact they help reduce damage to your self, the people spherical you, and the planet. By cultivating expertise via the observance of these precepts, you could navigate thru the chaos and uncertainty of lifestyles, finding a path to inner peace and harmony.

Let's take a better have a check the Five Precepts and find out how you could exercise them on your each day lifestyles:

Abstain from Taking Life (Killing):

Practice compassion and admire for all living beings, which includes animals and bugs. Reflect on the example of influential figures like Paul McCartney, who, inspired through his self-control to non-violence, have turn out to be a staunch suggest for animal rights and vegetarianism.

Abstain from Taking What is Not Given (Stealing):

Cultivate generosity and honesty, respecting the belongings and property of others. For instance, if confronted with the temptation to scouse borrow a person's concept or art work, remind yourself of the significance of integrity and try to provide credit score wherein it's due.

Abstain from Sexual Misconduct:

Honor your relationships and the relationships of others via being honest, responsible, and respectful in all romantic and sexual encounters. Recall the story of Keanu

Reeves, who has been praised for his respectful thoughts-set in the route of ladies, both on and off the set.

Abstain from False Speech (Lying):

Practice truthfulness and sincerity, being conscious of the consequences of your phrases. When confronted with a difficult situation, recollect the know-how of Abraham Lincoln, who as quickly as stated, "No man has a awesome sufficient reminiscence to be a a hit liar."

Abstain from Intoxicants that Cloud the Mind (Drugs and Alcohol):

Foster clarity and mindfulness, keeping off substances that could impair your judgment or bring about volatile moves.

1. Abstain from Taking Life (Killing)

One of the ways wherein proper movement is defined in Buddhism is thru the Five Precepts, which function a ethical compass guiding us in our interactions with the world. Let's delve into the primary of these precepts.

The first principle, often translated as "do now not wreck lifestyles," or "abstain from taking life," is ready fostering a deep recognize and compassion for all types of lifestyles. In the face of this principle, we are advised to apprehend the inherent rate of every living being and refrain from acts that would purpose harm or cease a existence.

This principle isn't quite a good buy warding off physical harm; it's additionally approximately now not causing emotional or intellectual damage to oneself or others. It encourages us to foster an thoughts-set of loving-kindness and compassion toward all beings, along with ourselves.

Consider the instance of the renowned film megastar and peace activist, Richard Gere. An ardent practitioner of Buddhism, Gere's self-discipline to the number one precept is plain in his humanitarian paintings, in particular in his advocacy for human rights in Tibet and his efforts to AIDS cognizance. Gere's existence is an embodiment of the compassionate movement entreated through this principle.

Abiding by way of way of this principle may additionally moreover have profound implications on your intellectual well-being too. When you commit to now not causing damage, you cultivate compassion and empathy, which can appreciably lessen emotions of anger, jealousy, and resentment, contributing for your internal peace and happiness.

Here is a easy mission listing that allow you to work out this principle for your everyday life:

Practice mindfulness to recognize and save you risky actions.

Cultivate empathy via seeking to apprehend the recollections and perspectives of others.

Engage in acts of kindness each day.

Reflect to your moves on the cease of the day and extensively recognized instances in which you succeeded in upholding the principle.

2. Abstain from Taking What is Not Given (Stealing)

"In giving freedom to the slave, we assure freedom to the unfastened - honorable alike in what we deliver, and what we preserve." These terms through Abraham Lincoln remind us of the profound implications of the second one principle of Buddhism - do now not scouse borrow.

Stealing, in its simplest shape, is taking what does not belong to us. This second principle urges us to chorus from such acts, cultivating respect for the rights and possessions of others. But it's now not pretty a whole lot the physical act of stealing. It moreover encompasses deceit, fraud, and another movements that control others for our gain.

Here are some methods you could exercising this precept:

Be honest in all of your dealings, ensuring you offer credit wherein it's due.

Respect the property of others and ask for permission in advance than using someone else's possessions.

Practice integrity, retaining your word, and high-quality your guarantees.

Just just like the first principle, the second one, too, has great implications in your intellectual nicely-being. When you exercise honesty and integrity, you nurture self-recognize and peace of mind. You now not deliver the burden of guilt or worry of being determined out, major to a experience of inner freedom and calmness.

three. Abstain from Sexual Misconduct

Sexual misconduct, in the Buddhist context, is greater than just a mandate in opposition to illicit or volatile sexual behavior. It's a call for us to recognize the sacredness of our our bodies and the our our bodies of others, and to act with integrity and hobby in all subjects of intimacy. By adhering to this principle, we foster accept as true with, appreciate, and peace internal our relationships, and we contribute to a extra healthful, more harmonious society.

Think approximately it this way - even as you're conscious of your moves, you're much less probably to cause harm to your self or others. This precept holds real in different factors of life, at the side of your intimate relationships. Just as you exercising mindfulness in deciding on your terms to prevent inflicting emotional ache, you need to recollect of your actions to save you inflicting harm on your romantic and sexual relationships.

In the overall public eye, we often see the bad influences of sexual misconduct executed out. Celebrity scandals, accusations, and the downfall of careers function stark reminders of the effects of now not adhering to this precept. Yet, there are also super figures who shine a moderate at the course of recognize and dignity.

So, how are you going to take a look at this precept on your personal lifestyles?

Firstly, be smooth about your intentions in any dating. Honesty and openness pave the manner for mutual facts and respect. Secondly, continuously are seeking out consent. Consent is the cornerstone of any wholesome and respectful sexual relationship. And thirdly, understand the limits set via others. Everyone has a right to their private area and luxury level.

four. Abstain from False Speech (Lying)

A lie, whether or not it takes the shape of a apparently innocent white lie or a fabricated tale supposed to protect any man or woman, creates boundaries that separate us from truth and distance us from the humans in our lives. When we lie, we create a fictional international that could appear convenient inside the short time period but can reason an internet of headaches and misunderstandings in the long run.

The precept of abstaining from lying isn't always pretty loads refraining from falsehoods; it's approximately cultivating a love for fact, in all its paperwork. It's approximately being real for your words, actual for your moves, and specially, real to yourself. It's approximately living authentically.

Here are some techniques you may encompass this precept:

Strive for honesty in all your communications.

Practice authenticity, being real on your emotions, mind, and ideals.

Avoid gossip and rumors, which regularly perpetuate untruths.

Following this precept contributes extensively to highbrow peace. When you speak and live your truth, you unburden yourself from the stress of keeping untruths. You foster trust in your relationships, and most importantly, you construct arrogance, know-how that you're living authentically.

5. Do Not Become Intoxicated

"Happiness isn't some component organized-made. It comes out of your very personal actions," the Dalai Lama as speedy as said. His words are a fitting segue into our exploration of the 5th precept of Buddhism: Do not end up intoxicated.

Chapter 3: The Five Hindrances

"Life is a chain of natural and spontaneous changes. Don't resist them; that nice creates sorrow. Let truth be truth. Let matters waft obviously ahead in anything way they prefer, " Lao Tzu. This quote perfectly encapsulates the essence of the Five Hindrances in Buddhism. These limitations as described below, are:

Doubt

Desire

Ill Will

Anxiousness and Worry

Sloth and Torpor (or Laziness and Lethargy)

Doubt

The first of the Five Hindrances in Buddhism, Doubt, is a fascinating undertaking to delve into. It's a few issue that everyone have professional subsequently in our lives. It's that nagging voice on your head, thinking the course you're on, the alternatives you've made, or even the ideals you maintain highly-priced.

The doubt we speak of in Buddhism is not the sort that encourages crucial questioning or self-mirrored picture. It is the sort that causes us to question the training of the Buddha, the course to enlightenment, and our very very own capability to reap it. It's a crippling uncertainty that leaves us stuck, not able to transport earlier on our non secular journey.

You see, doubt has this uncanny capability to creep into our minds, frequently neglected. It's like a fog that rolls in, obscuring our imaginative and prescient and inflicting us to lose sight of our vacation spot. It's a predicament that could without difficulty derail our religious development if left unchecked.

Take, for example, the story of Thomas Edison. Edison grow to be a prolific inventor, defensive 1,093 patents for his innovations. Yet, his journey become not with out traumatic conditions. His most superb invention, the electric mild bulb, took him 1,000 tries earlier than he in the end succeeded. Now, take into account if Edison had succumbed to doubt on his 999th try. We may additionally nonetheless be dwelling in a global lit with the useful aid of candlelight!

In Buddhism, overcoming doubt doesn't suggest blind faith. It way growing a deep information of the lessons and seeing their reality thru your private enjoy. It's approximately locating your personal proof of the direction's efficacy.

Desire

Desire, in its purest form, is a powerful motivator. It's the riding stress that propels us to chase our goals, try for success, and are seeking fulfillment in our lives. However, even as desire becomes unbalanced or misdirected, it can transform proper right into a hassle, a stumbling block on our direction to spiritual boom and enlightenment. This is especially right in the context of Buddhism, in which desire is taken into consideration one of the Five Hindrances to non secular improvement.

It's a thirst for some element that isn't always present, a longing for some thing more. This craving can manifest in plenty of office work, from fabric possessions to relationships, recognition, or stories. When we're stuck inside the grip of tanha, we're continuously searching for success outside of ourselves, believing that the following advertising, the following purchase, or the subsequent courting will in the end bring us the happiness we're seeking for.

However, the fact is that this form of choice handiest results in suffering. It's like a mirage within the wilderness, always performing without a doubt out of gain, no matter how a long way we excursion. The extra we chase after it, the extra it eludes us. This is the primary problem on the course to enlightenment in Buddhism.

So, how are we able to conquer this disadvantage? The solution lies in data the man or woman of desire and analyzing to navigate it with facts and mindfulness.

First, it's essential to apprehend that preference, in and of itself, isn't always inherently bad. It's a herbal part of the human revel in. The trouble arises while our dreams come to be attachments, main us to understand our happiness as contingent on outdoor possessions or conditions.

To overcome this, we need to learn how to cultivate non-attachment. This doesn't suggest that we ought to abandon all our goals and live a life with out ambition or enjoyment. Rather, it method getting to know to maintain our desires gently, understanding that they are no longer the deliver of our happiness.

Practicing mindfulness may be a effective tool on this device. When we're aware, we're virtually present within the second, not misplaced in mind approximately the past or the destiny. This permits us to look our goals for what they honestly are: short thoughts and feelings that come and float. We can look at them with out getting stuck up in them, with out letting them dictate our actions or our feel of self esteem.

Let's take a 2nd to mirror in this with a easy mindfulness exercise:

Take a few deep breaths, bringing your interest to the prevailing 2d.

Bring to thoughts a preference that you've been suffering with recently.

Observe this desire with out judgment. Notice the manner it feels on your body. What thoughts or emotions does it deliver up?

Remind yourself that this preference isn't you. It's only a concept, a feeling. It doesn't outline or manage you.

Let bypass of the selection, allowing it to bypass like a cloud inside the sky.

Ill Will

Ill will, the subsequent of the Five Hindrances in Buddhism, is some different impediment that we must look at to triumph over on our journey closer to enlightenment. This emotion, that may seem as anger, resentment, or hostility, acts as a effective roadblock, preventing us from experiencing the peace and tranquility that embody mindfulness and meditation.

Let's undergo in mind a real-global example. Remember the well-known feud amongst Steve Jobs and Bill Gates? These titans of era, each geniuses in their very very own proper, allowed their competition to make bigger into private animosity. This sick will not satisfactory added on them personal misery however additionally prompted neglected opportunities for collaboration that could have in addition revolutionized the tech world.

Such is the strength of sick will. It blinds us to opportunities, isolates us from others, and keeps us stuck in a cycle of negativity.

But the fine records is, we are able to triumph over it. Here's how:

Practice mindfulness: By turning into extra aware of your mind and emotions, you can become aware about sick will because it arises and choose no longer to interact with it.

Develop compassion: Instead of responding to others with anger or hostility, try to understand their attitude and respond with kindness.

Forgive: Holding onto grudges handiest fuels ill will. By forgiving others—and yourself—you could allow drift of horrible feelings and go with the flow in advance.

Cultivate positivity: Make a conscious effort to awareness on the good in others and in yourself. This can help counteract the negativity that includes unwell will.

Meditate: Regular meditation can help you control lousy feelings and cultivate a feel of internal peace.

Anxiousness and Worry

Anxiety and worry, the penultimate of the Five Hindrances, regularly stir up a typhoon in our minds and can be in particular tough to overcome. I'd want to percent a non-public story that could resonate with you. There have become a period in my lifestyles whilst the future modified into uncertain, and my thoughts modified into packed with a whirlwind of "what ifs" and worst-case eventualities. I involved regularly, losing valuable sleep and peace of thoughts. It changed into in some unspecified time in the future of this time that I recognized the profound keep tension and worry had over me.

You may also moreover additionally have professional this too. Perhaps you've located your self mendacity huge wakeful at night time time, fretting over an upcoming event or an unresolved hassle. Or probably your thoughts often races with troubles approximately the future, to the quantity which you warfare to be present in the moment.

Anxiousness and worry can form a powerful barrier to our spiritual improvement. They disturb our peace of mind, create unnecessary strain, and save you us from actually appealing with our meditation exercising. However, similar to the different Hindrances, they're no longer insurmountable boundaries however traumatic conditions to be understood and conquer.

Here's a list summarizing a few strategies to assist manage tension and fear:

Observing our mind and emotions without judgment through mindfulness can help us keep away from attractive with worry.

Intentionally focusing on best mind and feelings can counterbalance negativity brought about thru fear.

Exercise can lessen tension and promote nicely-being.

Seeking assist from trusted individuals or intellectual fitness professionals can offer beneficial coping strategies and attitude.

Regular meditation can beautify our ability to live gift and keep away from getting over excited thru worrying thoughts.

Let's recall the Buddha's phrases: "There isn't any direction to happiness: happiness is the course." Anxiousness and fear may be seen as instructors in location of enemies, supporting us apprehend the regions in our lives that need attention or trade. They offer us with the possibility to domesticate staying power, resilience, and compassion in the direction of ourselves.

Sloth and Torpor (Laziness and Lethargy)

These roadblocks can be mainly insidious as they subtly sap our electricity and motivation, preventing us from sincerely attractive with our meditation exercise and lifestyles itself.

Remember the story of the tortoise and the hare? The hare, regardless of being the quicker and additional succesful animal, loses the race because of the fact he chooses to relaxation and procrastinate, on the identical time because the tortoise, despite the fact that slower, wins due to his ordinary attempt and refusal to succumb to laziness. In the equal way, we often have all the abilties and abilities we want to gain our non secular dreams, but we are held lower returned through our non-public inertia.

Sloth and torpor can appear in diverse strategies. We may additionally additionally locate ourselves feeling bodily slow, mentally foggy, or emotionally tired. We may moreover start heading off our meditation workout or locate our minds wandering aimlessly whilst we do try to meditate. These are all signs that sloth and torpor have crept in.

The properly facts is, we are not powerless against those stumbling blocks.

Here's how you may deal with them:

Set smooth dreams: Having a smooth vision of what we need to obtain can assist us live inspired and targeted.

Establish a habitual: Regular workout can assist us assemble momentum and make it much less complex to live with our meditation.

Take care of our physical health: Regular workout, a healthy eating regimen, and sufficient sleep can help hold our energy tiers excessive.

Seek assist: Joining a meditation enterprise or finding a mentor can offer us with the encouragement and duty we want.

Practice mindfulness: By being aware about our mind and emotions, we can phrase at the same time as sloth and torpor begin to creep in and take steps to counteract them.

THE FOUR IMMEASURABLES

The Four Immeasurables:

Loving-Kindness

Compassion

Sympathetic Joy

Equanimity

"Thousands of candles can be lighted from a unmarried candle, and the existence of the candle will now not be shortened. Happiness in no manner decreases thru manner of being shared." — Buddha

Loving-Kindness (Metta)

It emerge as on a chilly wintry weather's day at the same time as I changed into huddled within the warm temperature of my take a look at that I acquired an e mail. It become from an entire stranger living midway throughout the globe. The message grow to be easy, "I preference this e mail unearths you nicely. I just wanted to say I respect your work and I choice you have were given got a adorable day." This small act of kindness is a lovable instance of the Buddhist idea of Metta, also referred to as loving-kindness.

Metta is a Pali time period that doesn't have an actual English identical, but it could be defined as benevolent kindness toward all beings with out exception. It's now not selective; it doesn't differentiate between a pal, an enemy, or a stranger. Metta is a boundless, time-venerated love — an aspiration, a performance of the coronary coronary heart.

When we domesticate Metta internal ourselves, we start to dissolve the limitations that we've erected because of fear, jealousy, or hatred. We start to see beyond the labels of 'pal', 'enemy', or 'stranger'. We begin to choice for the nicely-being of all lifestyles paperwork, irrespective of who they're, in which they arrive from, or what they've finished. This might also sound like a Herculean undertaking, but it's instead natural as fast as we start working towards it.

Here's a clean Metta meditation exercise you can start with:

Find a quiet area and take a seat with out difficulty.

Close your eyes and take some deep breaths to center your self.

Begin with the useful resource of directing Metta towards your self. Silently repeat, "May I be satisfied. May I be wholesome. May I be safe. May I stay without difficulty."

Next, keep in mind someone you need. Direct the identical desires in the route of them.

Think of a unbiased person, someone you neither like nor dislike. Extend the equal wants to them.

Now, reflect onconsideration on a person with whom you have got were given a hard courting. If you're prepared, attempt extending Metta to them as nicely.

Finally, expand this choice to all beings anywhere, "May all beings be glad. May all beings be healthful. May all beings be stable. May all beings live pretty really."

This workout won't be easy earlier than the whole thing, specially on the same time as directing Metta toward humans we've got were given troubles with. But keep in thoughts, Metta is a exercise. It's like exercise a muscle. The more we do it, the more potent it turns into.

Cultivating Metta is a effective way to transform our hearts and minds. It permits us to move from a area of separateness and worry to a area of connectedness and love. It's the first step closer to embracing the four immeasurable tendencies which can be the foundation of a in reality enriched life.

Compassion (Karuna)

"Compassion is not a gesture of the inclined, however the fortitude of the sturdy." This quote from the renowned Buddhist monk, Matthieu Ricard, perfectly encapsulates the essence of compassion, or Karuna, in Buddhism. It's a cornerstone of our exercising, and it isn't always certainly approximately feeling sorry for others; it's about the profound preference to relieve struggling wherever it exists. Let's delve into this immeasurable element and apprehend how it is able to transform your life and intellectual properly-being.

Compassion (Karuna), in its exceptional phrases, is the coronary coronary coronary heart's reaction to struggling. It's the empathetic knowledge that perceives the battle of others and wants to alleviate it. But compassion isn't quite lots acknowledging ache and suffering. It moreover includes a dedication to taking motion to alleviate it. When we domesticate compassion, we're not only acknowledging the everyday fact of struggling however additionally committing ourselves to alleviate it.

In my private journey with Buddhism, I've observed that cultivating compassion isn't commonly smooth, mainly whilst we stumble upon human beings or conditions that venture our staying power and understanding. Yet, it's within the ones moments that compassion turns into an invaluable device for non-public transformation and peace.

This is the transformative strength of compassion. It no longer best adjustments our perspective but moreover alters our reactions, principal to more peace and equanimity in our lives.

But how are you going to domesticate such compassion? Here's a practical guide to help you:

Mindfulness: Start by the usage of schooling mindfulness. Be simply determined in each second and permit yourself to truly recognize the evaluations and emotions of others.

Empathy: Try to understand the feelings and views of others. Put yourself of their shoes and attempt to sense what they'll be feeling. This understanding is the first step within the course of growing compassion.

Action: Compassion consists of more than just know-how; it additionally calls for movement.

Look for strategies to relieve the struggling of others, whether or not or now not or not it's lending a listening ear, imparting assist, or honestly being there for them.

Meditation: Compassion meditation, moreover called Metta or Loving-Kindness Meditation, is a powerful device for cultivating compassion. It involves consciously sending goals of nicely-being, happiness, and peace to all beings.

"When you start to touch your coronary coronary heart or allow your heart be touched, you start to discover that it's bottomless, that it doesn't have any decision, that this coronary heart is huge, large, and limitless. You begin to find out how loads warm temperature and gentleness is there, similarly to how masses region." - Pema Chödrön.

Compassion, in essence, is prepared beginning our hearts to the suffering of others and ourselves. It's approximately acknowledging this suffering and taking steps to alleviate it. As you stroll this course of compassion, you'll discover a profound feel of peace and fulfillment pervading your life, reworking your evaluations and interactions in awesome strategies. Remember, compassion isn't just for the advantage of others; it's further for our very own mental and emotional well-being. Embrace Karuna and permit its transformative power manual you for your path to enlightenment.

Sympathetic Joy (Mudita)

The Dalai Lama as soon as stated, "If you want others to be happy, workout compassion. If you need to be happy, exercising compassion." But there's each other detail of Buddhist philosophy that contributes to happiness, each ours and that of others, and that's sympathetic satisfaction, or Mudita.

Sympathetic delight is the real joy we sense at the happiness and fulfillment of others. It's the capability to take honest satisfaction inside the achievements, nicely-being, and delight of others, with out a touch of jealousy or resentment. It's about celebrating others as we'd have fun our private success.

But why is Mudita so vital? Well, it's because it allows us escape the trap of jealousy and resentment. These bad emotions no longer pleasant cloud our minds however moreover bring about a huge amount of struggling. By cultivating Mudita, we are able to permit move of these damaging feelings and update them with happiness and contentment.

Now, you is probably wondering, "That sounds excellent, however how do I in truth practice Mudita?" The solution lies in mindfulness, empathy, and aware strive.

Here's a simple manual to help you get commenced out:

Chapter 4: Meditation And Mindfulness

Meditation

" Life is a dance. Mindfulness is witnessing that dance ." - Amit Ray. Let's take a 2d to mirror in this quote. It's a clean however profound declaration that captures the essence of meditation. Now, permit's discover the transformative strength of meditation inside the context of Buddhism.

Meditation is not handiest a exercise; it's a adventure, a path to self-discovery. It's like a mirror that displays our internal selves, assisting us understand who we without a doubt are. It's a tool that enables us navigate the tumultuous seas of lifestyles with grace and equanimity.

Shinzen Young, a renowned meditation teacher, fairly encapsulates the benefits of aware meditation into 3 center factors: sensory readability, focus, and equanimity. Let's delve a hint deeper into every of these.

Sensory readability is prepared being absolutely privy to what we're experiencing inside the present 2d. It's approximately tuning into our senses and staring at our mind, feelings, and bodily sensations with out judgment. It's like turning up the amount on life, experiencing it in excessive-definition.

Concentration, rather, is ready recognition. It's about schooling our minds to stay in the gift 2d, no longer getting misplaced inside the beyond or the future. It's about cultivating a experience of stillness amidst the chaos of life.

Equanimity is probably the maximum profound of the three. It's approximately developing a balanced thoughts, a thoughts that remains undisturbed in the face of existence's americaand downs. It's about gaining knowledge of to experience the waves of lifestyles with grace and poise.

Now, permit's take a step decrease back and take a look at the larger photograph. In the grand tapestry of Buddhism, meditation is a colorful thread that weaves thru its philosophical device. It's an antidote to the nagging troubles of ego, a pathway to transformation. It's a beacon of moderate for those trying to find to live a lifestyles freed from greed, hate, and phantasm.

In the Pali canon, the Buddha outlines meditative traits which can be jointly supportive: samatha, or "calm," and vipassanā, or "perception." Picture those functions as a pair of fast messengers, working in concord to supply the profound message of Nirvana.

Samatha, the primary messenger, brings calm. It's like a calming balm for our restless minds, assisting us cultivate a feel of peace and calmness. Vipassanā, the second one messenger, brings belief. It's like a pointy sword that cuts thru the veil of lack of information, helping us see truth as it honestly is.

Together, those messengers supply the profound message of nirvana, the closing motive of Buddhism. Nirvana is not a place but a kingdom of mind. It's a country of profound peace and happiness, free from the shackles of greed, hate, and fable.

Now, allow's take this data and positioned it into workout.

Here's a easy mindfulness workout to get you commenced:

Find a quiet place in that you obtained't be disturbed.

Sit with out difficulty, together with your lower lower back proper away but no longer stiff.

Close your eyes and take a few deep breaths.

Bring your hobby on your breath. Notice the sensation of the breath coming in and going out.

If your mind wanders, gently deliver it decrease back to the breath.

Continue this practice for a couple of minutes every day.

Remember, meditation is not approximately accomplishing a tremendous nation or having a particular revel in. It's approximately being gift, being simply engaged with some issue goes on right now. It's approximately cultivating a sense of curiosity and openness in the course of our very very own revel in.

Some Forms of Meditation

Here's the factor: meditation isn't just about sitting pass-legged on a mat, murmuring 'Om' in a low voice till your throat dries up. No, meditation is a lot more severa and interesting than you would possibly think. And I'm going to stroll you through a few types of meditation which can be as soothing as a warm cup of chamomile tea on a frosty wintry weather night time time.

First on the listing is Vipassanā. Originating from the land of the Buddha, Vipassanā is one of the maximum historic forms of meditation.

It specializes in seeing topics as they definitely are. It's all about looking at the fact inside your self, and permit me let you recognise, when you start peeling back those layers, it's like locating a in no manner-completing Russian nesting doll!

Next, we have Samatha. If you trust you studied this seems like a mild, soothing lullaby, you're no longer some distance off. This form of meditation entails calming the mind and its 'formations.' It's like giving your thoughts a tranquilizer so you can experience peace. It ought to probable seem a chunk hard inside the beginning, however when you get the hold of it, it's smoother than a hot knife via butter.

Following Samatha, we've Mantra Meditation. This shape of meditation makes use of a repeated sound, word, or phrase to clean the mind. Imagine you're within the serene valleys of Tibet, surrounded by means of way of the usage of lush greenery, and you're chanting "Om mani padme hum," which loosely translates to "Hail to the jewel within the lotus." Believe me, it's a cathartic revel in that definitely melts away your strain.

Next, we've Metta Meditation, moreover called Loving-Kindness Meditation. This shape of meditation is all about directing suitable vibes closer to your self and others. It's like sending out a boomerang of affection and satisfactory power and looking it circle over again to you.

Lastly, there's Chanting, Visualization, and Walking Meditations. Each gives a first-rate flavor, much like plenty of chocolates in a field. Chanting is all about the usage of rhythmic spoken or sung phrases to get right right into a meditative kingdom. Visualization is like taking vicinity a highbrow excursion, developing serene pix on your mind, and strolling meditation is ready being privy to each step and every breath at the same time as taking a non violent stroll.

Here's a chunk workout for you. I need you to pick out out one form of meditation from the list above that resonates with you the most. Try operating closer to it for five mins each day for the following week. Write down any modifications or emotions you look at in your thoughts, behavior, or emotions in a magazine. This exercise will not best give you a hands-on experience with meditation however additionally give you insight into the way it impacts you.

I can permit you to understand from personal experience that the effect of meditation is like which includes a hint of colourful colour to a black and white portray. It's the greater seasoning in the soup of existence that complements its flavor and makes it nicely nicely worth savoring. And the splendor of it all? Anyone can discover ways to meditate - it's as elegant because of the truth the air we breathe, the water we drink, and the love we percentage.

Meditation Equipment

"Tools make the person," so is going a cutting-edge version of a proverb. But on the subject of meditation, I am inclined to make a slight change: "The loss of tools ought to make the person, however having them doesn't damage." Let me give an explanation for.

As we embark on the adventure into the serene international of Buddhism, it is essential to maintain in mind that meditation is a sojourn of the thoughts. It does now not usually require physical tool. But really as a wanderer appreciates a map or a compass, there are fantastic tools, historically used by many working in the direction of Buddhists, that would decorate your meditation enjoy. However, the ones range some of the numerous schools of Buddhism and are not conditions. You see, meditation is a no-frills affair; it's like showing as a whole lot as a potluck with virtually your urge for meals!

Now, for the ones of you who like a chunk extra, allow's dive into this charming array of meditation gadget.

1. A Meditation Cushion (Zafu)

Imagine being within the center of a deeply profound meditation consultation, however all you can focus on is your sore bottom. That's wherein the Zafu is available in! This meditation cushion, often full of kapok or buckwheat, gives a soft and stable platform in an effort to perch upon. It's like sitting on a cloud, without the priority of falling via!

2. Incense

Incense sticks have a alternatively old skool and realistic use in meditation - they function timers. In the antique days, meditators can also need to start their session while the incense come to be lit and can understand it have turn out to be time to wrap up even as the candy-smelling smoke stopped wafting through the air. It's like a slight, olfactory faucet at the shoulder, reminding you of the world outside your thoughts. Plus, the aroma can assist create a relaxing surroundings.

3. Timer, Bell, or Tibetan Singing Bowl

Timers, bells, and Tibetan developing a tune bowls create an auditory backdrop for meditation. Like a moderate ripple breaking the floor of a peaceful lake, the resonating sound of these gadgets serves as a sonic marker for the start and end of your meditation session.

4. Altar and Altar Cloth

An altar adorned with a totally unique fabric can function a seen reminder of your willpower to workout. It is a touch nook in your own home dedicated to your non secular adventure, a steady reminder of the tranquil direction you have got chosen.

5. Candles and Flowers

In the dance of shadows cast with the useful resource of a flickering candle, we see the photo of the mild of reality, guiding us through obscurity. Similarly, plant life, in their ephemeral splendor, remind us of the impermanence of nature. Together, they form a compelling, tactile metaphor for some of the important teachings of Buddhism.

6. Devotional Objects

Statues of Buddha or particular devotional devices to your altar can characteristic focal factors at some point of meditation. They represent the enlightened america you aspire to obtain. It's like having a photo of your excursion spot, a moderate nudge reminding you of your adventure's motive.

7. Prayer Beads

Finally, prayer beads, frequently carved from the wood of the Bodhi tree. A strand usually consists of 108 beads and is used within the exercising of Japa, in which you repeat a mantra, like "Om mani padme hum." The beads help you preserve track of the quantity of repetitions, like a religious abacus.

Now, right right here's a touch workout for you:

Create a area for meditation in your property, the usage of any of the gadgets cited above that resonate with you. Don't be troubled if you can't get all of them - take into account, the most critical tool for meditation is your thoughts. This setup is definitely a way to decorate your revel in.

Posture

Ah, posture! It's a deceptively clean concept, isn't it? We've all been admonished as youngsters to "Sit up right now!" But who knew that this reputedly mundane directive have to evolve into an complicated dance with profound implications for the thoughts, body, and spirit?

As we delve into meditation, it's important to apprehend that posture isn't about inflexible adherence to an esoteric protocol, however as an alternative an understanding of our our our bodies and the interconnectedness of our physical and intellectual properly-being. In the area of meditation, the body isn't always surely a automobile, but an active participant in the adventure to inner peace.

Let's start with a story. Once upon a time, in my early days of studying about Buddhism and meditation, I became happy that I had to keep near the entire lotus posture. You recognise the simplest - with each toes resting at the possibility thigh, like a pretzel. The satisfactory hassle modified into that my body, being extra acquainted with ergonomic place of business chairs and highly-priced sofas, did not pretty agree. The extra tough I tried, the more my knees screamed for mercy. It have come to be quite the standoff, my stubbornness closer to my frame's unwillingness to bend to my will. I positioned a important lesson from this revel in: the adventure closer to mindfulness starts offevolved with being attentive to our our our bodies, respecting their obstacles, and meeting them wherein they're.

So, allow's discover some postures that may be more agreeable to your knees, we could?

The complete lotus: It's the vital meditation pose, with each foot resting on the alternative thigh. It's first-rate for balance and alignment, but be warned, it's now not for absolutely everyone, and that's ok!

The half-lotus: This one is a piece an awful lot much less pretzel-like. One foot rests on the opposite thigh, and the possibility rests below the thigh. It's a bit an awful lot less tough however even though gives nicely stability.

The Burmese fashion: This is the grounded version of the lotus. Both ft relaxation on the ground within the front of you, with one leg in the the front of the possibility. It's cushty and virtually accommodating for people who, like me, have bodies that draw the street at pretzel impersonations.

Seated on a proper away-subsidized chair: This one is for the rebels who refuse to sit down at the ground. Make high-quality your ft contact the floor, your once more is directly however now not rigid, and your fingers resting in your knees or lap.

Remember that the great posture is the one in which you may keep a right now but comfortable again, and your body isn't distracting you with proceedings of ache. It ought to permit you, not restriction you.

Now, here's a beneficial tip. Doing some mild stretching earlier than settling into your posture must make a international of distinction. It's like giving your body a heads-up, "Hey, we're approximately to try this mindfulness aspect." This now not handiest enables to prevent soreness but also serves as a transition ritual, a bridge from the hustle and bustle of each day existence to the calm region of meditation.

Lastly, do not forget to understand your body and its limits. Just as there can be no person 'right' manner to are looking for internal peace, there may be no person 'right' posture. It's a non-public journey, and the suitable posture is the simplest that permits you to journey the direction of mindfulness with consolation and dignity. Your body is your companion in this journey, and prefer all pinnacle partners, it merits to be heard and respected.

Alright, now that you've had this crash course in meditation posture, I wish you revel in organized to sit down (without a doubt) collectively with your exercising. Remember, the simplest 'lousy' meditation posture is the simplest that reasons you discomfort or harm. Your body is smart. Listen to it, and it will manual you well.

Environment

Ah, there's no vicinity like domestic. Or is there? Home, office, outside - wherever you are, a tranquil surroundings must make all the distinction in your day. Especially whilst you're trying to meditate. In fact, it's highly essential. Let me supply an cause of. Picture this: you're meditating, zenning out, whilst , a loud car honks out of doors your window. Or worse, your smartphone buzzes with each distinct notification. It's like a person splashing bloodless water in your face on the equal time as you're in a heat, soothing bath.

So, permit's make your environment meditation-friendly. First topics first, find out a quiet spot wherein the chaos of the area can't interfere. This can be a corner in your home, a snug corner for your place of job, or perhaps a park bench. It's not lots approximately where you're, as it is about the peace the region can offer.

But even within the quietest corners, time has a sneaky manner of slipping a long way from us, doesn't it? One minute, you're taking deep, calming breaths, and the subsequent, you're questioning if you've been sitting there for an eternity. So, right right here's a on hand tip - set a time restrict. Maybe you start with ten minutes, like dipping your feet proper right right into a pool to check the waters. Then, as you extend extra snug and your attention improves, you could grade by grade growth this restriction.

Now, on the subject of timers, I need you to expect the maximum abrupt, jarring alarm you've ever heard. Got it? Great. Now forget about approximately it. You're now not the use of that to your meditation. Instead, find out a sound that is as gentle and soothing as a lullaby. Trust me, you don't want to be jolted out of your serene state.

One closing trouble - while your timer does in the end sing its smooth melody, don't just bounce up. Remember, you've been sitting for a while. Your legs might be a bit stiff or maybe asleep. So, take it slow. Stand up slowly, and shake out your legs. There's no rush. You're in the zen location now, recollect?

Here's a bit greater some factor you may do. Just as you're about to forestall your meditation session, you may perform a smooth act of honor - a bow. It can be a bodily one, or only for your coronary coronary heart. It's a second of reverence for the exercise you've without a doubt completed.

Your meditation environment is similar to your thoughts - it ought to be non violent, with out distractions, and conducive to mindfulness. Now pass on, make that best location for yourself. Your future zen-self will thank you.

The Breath

Can I proportion a hint mystery with you? It's some thing anyone proportion, some component that's right below our noses (virtually!) - but, we regularly forget it.

Yes, it's your breath.

Your breath is one of the most reliable allies you can have for your journey of existence. Always there, faithfully following your rhythm, in sorrow and pleasure, in haste and rest. It's the maximum reliable partner you could ever preference for. Yet, we barely be aware of it. In our rapid-paced lives, in which we continuously juggle paintings, own family, and that seemingly in no manner-finishing to-do list, it's easy to forget about approximately this ever-present partner.

Consider this example: You're frantically racing via your day, and you sense the sector spinning round you. Your coronary heart's pounding, you're gasping for breath, panic creeping in. In those moments, you understand the power of your breath, and also you gasp, trying to attraction to more air. That's whilst your breath says, "Hey there, I've been proper here all alongside, actually breathe!"

Just like a trusty pal who pulls you apart and says, "Take a moment, breathe, the entirety's going to be ok," your breath is constantly there for you. You want best flip your recognition to it.

In the training of Buddhism, the eye of breath performs a critical function. It office work the foundation of Buddhist-fashion meditation, allowing you to anchor your cognizance and find out a ordinary place amidst the typhoon of mind and emotions. Breath, in Buddhism, is greater than a physical way; it's a metaphorical bridge connecting your body and mind.

Now, there are as many techniques to attention at the breath as there are to cook dinner dinner an egg (and take delivery of as real with me, that's quite some). From pranayama, this is a part of the yogic tradition, to Zazen, the Zen meditation style, to Anapanasati, which means that that that mindfulness of inhaling Pali - the historic language of early Buddhist scriptures.

Pranayama is a Sanskrit word that interprets to "lifestyles-pressure manipulate." It consists of various techniques that have an effect on the flow of strength on your frame thru controlling your breath. In assessment, Zazen, which means that "seated meditation" in Japanese, is the exercise of attempting to find the "simply sitting" kingdom, wherein your breath will become your focal factor of recognition. Then there's Anapanasati, a exercising that Buddha himself is stated to have taught. In this technique, your focus is on the sensations of respiratory, looking at it with out seeking to manipulate it.

Regardless of the approach you pick out, the ones strategies percentage a commonplace intention - improving your recognition and statistics of your breath. By harnessing the electricity of your breath, you can faucet into the tranquility it offers, thereby bringing peace and calmness for your chaotic life.

For starters, permit's take a easy exercise. Wherever you're, a few issue you're doing, pause for a 2nd. Now, near your eyes, take a gradual, deep breath in, preserve it for a second, and then exhale slowly. Repeat this for a few greater breaths. As you achieve this, take a look at your breath - experience the cool air coming into your nostrils, your chest increasing, after which the pleasant and relaxed air leaving your body.

How did that experience? Simple, wasn't it? That's the strength of breath focus. It doesn't need any fancy props or devoted time. You can do it proper here, proper now.

Mindfulness

Mindfulness. What a treasure trove it holds internal! You've heard the time period thrown round before, haven't you? Perhaps, inside the midst of your frenetic normal rush, it got here to you as echo, a whisper of a higher way. Or possibly you heard it ultimately of your short ventures into the world of self-development, nestled snugly among guarantees of tranquility, pressure relief, and that elusive unicorn – happiness. But what is mindfulness certainly? And what does it ought to do with emotional intelligence and the principles of Buddhism? Well, we're approximately to embark on a adventure of discovery collectively to discover.

Chapter 5: Karma And Rebirth

Karma is not a difficult idea

Now, allow's dive into one of the most misunderstood standards in Buddhism: Karma.

You recognize, I frequently smile once I pay interest humans use the term "karma" in regular conversation. It's normally some component along the traces of, "Oh, that's karma for you!" whilst someone receives their honestly cakes. But karma is so much extra than cosmic payback.

In its simplest form, karma is the regulation of reason and effect. It's the idea that each motion has a impact, and these outcomes shape our lives. It's like throwing a pebble right right into a pond. The pebble is your motion, and the ripples it creates are the outcomes of that movement.

Understanding and the usage of the concept of karma is not as difficult because it appears. It's approximately being aware of our movements and their results on ourselves and others. It's approximately making conscious alternatives that bring about awesome outcomes.

Now, right here's a touch workout for you:

Over the subsequent week, I need you to pay near hobby on your movements and their results. Write them down in a magazine. At the surrender of the week, evaluation your entries. You is probably amazed at what you find.

Remember, karma isn't a punishment or praise. It's a tool for facts the interconnectedness of our moves and their outcomes. It's a direction to a extra mindful and compassionate life. And it's a route that's open to everyone.

Common Misunderstandings About Karma

First off, allow's treatment a not unusual false impression. Karma isn't always some cosmic scorekeeper, tallying up your actual and lousy deeds, prepared to reward or punish you for this reason. If you're imagining a celestial accountant with a massive ledger, erase that picture from your thoughts. Karma doesn't paintings that way.

Think of Karma as extra like a seed. Every motion you're taking is a seed you plant. Some seeds change into adorable plant life, others into thorny wooden. The shape of seed you plant, through your movements, will decide what grows in your lifestyles.

Now, I apprehend what you're wondering, "are you announcing if I do actual matters, simplest proper matters will take area to me?" Well, now not exactly. Life is complex, and so is Karma. It's not a one-to-one transaction. But typically, incredible moves create conditions for wonderful effects, and awful movements create conditions for terrible results.

But right here's the lovely detail about Karma. You can exchange the seeds you're planting. When I began out taking care of my health, meditating, and practicing mindfulness, I commenced planting seeds of self-care. And guess what? Those seeds grew proper into a lawn of well-being.

So, allow's strive a touch exercise:

Think about the seeds you're planting to your life proper now.

Are they seeds of kindness, compassion, and knowledge?

Or are they seeds of anger, resentment, and forget?

Remember, you have got the energy to choose what seeds you plant.

Here's a assignment list that will help you alongside the manner:

Identify the seeds: What moves are you taking for your lifestyles proper now? Are they splendid or terrible?

Choose your seeds: Decide what form of movements you need to take. What type of seeds do you need to plant?

Plant your seeds: Start taking those moves. Plant those seeds.

Nurture your seeds: Keep taking exceptional moves. Nurture the ones seeds with mindfulness and compassion.

Remember, Karma isn't always about punishment or praise. It's approximately facts the outcomes of our actions and making aware picks. It's approximately planting the seeds for the lifestyles we want to live.

Karma is an ethical compass to your life.

Imagine you're in a ship inside the middle of the sea. You don't have any map, no GPS, and no concept which manner to transport. You're out of place, right? But then, you recollect you have got were given a compass. Suddenly, you have got a course. You understand in which north is, and you could navigate your manner domestic.

That's what Karma may be in your lifestyles. It's no longer approximately worry of punishment or anticipation of reward. It's approximately having a revel in of course. It's approximately information that your actions depend variety and might manual you inside the course of a existence of peace, compassion, and records.

There had been times as soon as I felt like I become rowing in the direction of the current-day-day. It wasn't easy, but I stored going. I stored following my moral compass. And you understand what? It led me to an area of peace and know-how. It led me home.

So, how can you use Karma as an moral compass to your lifestyles? It starts offevolved with mindfulness. Pay interest to your actions and their outcomes. Are they inflicting damage or selling peace? Are they pushed by egocentric desires or compassionate intentions?

Try this exercise:

For the following week, attempt to undergo in mind of your actions.

At the prevent of each day, write down one movement which you're glad with and one motion that you expect you could decorate.

Reflect on the ones movements and their consequences.

This smooth workout will let you begin the use of Karma as an ethical compass for your lifestyles.

Remember, Karma isn't always a select. It's a manual. It's a compass that let you navigate the sea of life.

Karma and Rebirth

Rebirth in Buddhism isn't approximately coming lower returned as a one-of-a-type creature on your subsequent existence. It's now not a literal reincarnation. Instead, it's about the continuation of cognizance. Picture it like a flame passing from one candle to some different. The flame is the identical, but the candles are specific.

Karma and rebirth are sides of the identical coin. They're interconnected. The movements we absorb this existence (our Karma) have an effect at the person of our focus in the subsequent (our rebirth).

"Each morning we're born all over again. What we do in recent times subjects maximum." - Buddha. Isn't that a fascinating way to kickstart our day? Think approximately it for a second. You and I, we're generally being reborn, one 2nd at a time, inside the destiny at a time. In the grand scheme of things, it's what we choose out to do in recent times that shapes our tomorrow.

That's Karma for you, and as you may've guessed, it's tightly intertwined with rebirth. Now, in advance than you get visions of being reincarnated as a grasshopper or a raccoon, permit's delve a bit deeper into the ones requirements.

Let's speak approximately Karma first, the engine of reason and impact that drives our existence everyday with Buddhist philosophy.

Don't you discover it amusing that Karma has come to be this type of pop-manner of life buzzword? It's nearly like Karma has its very very very own advertising and advertising and marketing and advertising crew! But its reputation furthermore comes with a suitcase complete of misconceptions. So, let's unpack that suitcase and demystify Karma.

Karma, in its essence, is a fundamental law of the universe. It states that our actions, be they physical, verbal, or intellectual, go away an imprint on our mind so that it will always ripen into revel in at the identical time as the situations are right.

Imagine Karma because the maximum sophisticated 4D printer ever. You feed it with blueprints of your moves and thoughts, and it prints out corresponding testimonies for you. Feed it with real, healthy stuff, and voila! You get happy, extremely good critiques. Feed it with no longer-so-genuine stuff... Well, you recognize what takes area. It's just like the antique computer programming adage,

"Garbage in, rubbish out." Only that with Karma, it's greater like "top notch in, specific out" and "lousy in, terrible out."

That brings us to the second part of our speak, rebirth. Now, it's smooth to view rebirth as a form of divine recycling software, wherein we get a modern-day-day life form primarily based totally on our beyond moves. But Buddhism seems at rebirth from a greater nuanced attitude. It's not a easy be counted wide variety of taking a modern day start after lack of existence. It's approximately the non-stop cycle of beginning, demise, and rebirth.

Every second, each day, we're going via this cycle. We take actions, we are facing the consequences, after which we're reborn into the subsequent 2nd, carrying with us the baggage of our beyond. It's an ongoing approach, similar to the endless cycle of seasons or the relentless waves of the ocean.

Here's some other workout for you:

Try to spend an afternoon looking at your moves and thoughts, and the way they impact your temper, your interactions, and your studies. Don't choose out or trade anything, simply have a have a look at. You might be surprised at the insights you benefit approximately your very own cycle of karma and rebirth.

Now, this could all sound heavy and a bit overwhelming. But right here's the silver lining. Buddhists believe that we've the energy to exchange our Karma, and by using doing so, trade our experience of rebirth, 2nd thru way of 2nd, every day.

The Tibetan Book of the Dead: a traditional of Buddhist knowledge on dying and death

The Tibetan Book of the Dead, or Bardo Thodol, is a guide for the journey after death, however it's also a manual for the adventure of existence. It's about information the impermanence of existence, the cycle of loss of existence and rebirth, and the liberation that may be found in this knowledge.

Now, I can nearly pay attention you wondering, "This sounds a piece heavy for my morning coffee reading." And you're right. It's no longer light studying. But it's exceedingly enlightening (pun meant).

The Tibetan Book of the Dead teaches us that lack of existence is not an quit, but a transition. It's a continuation of the journey. This information can assist us stay our lives greater completely, understanding that every 2nd is valuable and fleeting.

So, how are you going to exercise this focus in your lifestyles? Start via way of using reflecting on the impermanence of life. Consider how this data would possibly probably trade your mindset on your each day reviews.

We all apprehend about loss of existence, that inevitable reality that visits every one parents subsequently. Still, dying is often a taboo, a frightened challenge depend tucked away in the yet again of our minds like an unwelcome guest. However, in Buddhism, death is a milestone, a transitional segment, a journey in itself. This notion resonates perfectly with the ancient Buddhist scripture called The Tibetan Book of the Dead. Today, we will adventure via its expertise.

Imagine you're trekking on a acquainted trail. You've been there endless instances, and you recognize the turns, dips, and elevations. But this time, you come across a formerly unseen fork within the direction. Two paths beckon, each with its specific landscape and intrigue. The first one is a properly-trodden direction, cushty however monotonous. The other, is a far less trodden path, mysterious and full of unknown wonders.

This situation is a metaphor for life and loss of life. The diagnosed direction represents life, the mysterious one symbolizes loss of existence. The Tibetan Book of the Dead introduces us to this unknown direction, illustrating the adventure beyond the bodily worldwide.

A profoundly transformative piece, the Tibetan Book of the Dead takes us into the "bardos," intermediate stages amongst life, loss of life, and rebirth. It gives an fantastic attitude at the cyclical nature of lifestyles, guiding the deceased and their loved ones thru the method of death and past.

Here's a simple workout to try:

Jot down what loss of lifestyles method to you.

Your thoughts, emotions, fears, or curiosities.

This easy exercising can function a reflect, reflecting your know-how and relationship with this inevitable transition.

Chapter 6: The Three Schools Of Buddhism

Let's dig into our journey of information Buddhism nowadays by using considering how the spread and development of this philosophy passed off after Lord Buddha's demise. Imagine the compassionate teachings of Lord Buddha, rippling out from the standard heartland of India, attaining a long manner corners of the region and embracing distinct cultures, traditions, and techniques of life. Just as water in a river need to glide, so too did Buddhism evolve, reminding us of Buddha's critical training, " Everything is situation to trade."

Theravāda or the School of the Elders

Around 250 BC, we see the emergence of Theravāda or the School of the Elders. The most orthodox shape of Buddhism, Theravāda positioned its adherents often in Southeast Asia, specially Sri Lanka (in which it unfold first, from India), Thailand, and Myanmar. Picture a serene temple tucked in a lush Sri

Lankan jungle, monks clad in saffron gowns chanting early within the morning due to the fact the day breaks, their teachings seeping into the very soil of the land. The cutting-edge Vipassana motion, and truely, the mindfulness craze proper proper here within the West, famous its roots interior Theravāda Buddhism. Isn't it superb that the ones teachings from over millennia in the beyond but resonate with us these days?

Mahāyāna, the Great Vehicle

Fast in advance to the first century BC, and the level is ready for Mahāyāna, the Great Vehicle, to make its grand front. With lovers predominantly discovered in China, Japan, and Korea, Mahāyāna emerged with its specific tendencies. Imagine the Zen gardens of Japan or the grandiose halls of a Chinese temple complete of a profound, echoey silence. Zen and Pure Land are schools of idea that this way of life birthed, reminding us of the variety within Buddhism itself.

Vajrayāna, the Diamond Vehicle

Enter the 5th century AD, and we witness the delivery of Vajrayāna, the Diamond Vehicle, it is a glittery offshoot of Mahāyāna. If you have got been to go to Tibet throughout the 7th century AD, you'd see a model of this school flourishing, known as Tibetan Buddhism. Imagine the melodic hum of mantras echoing throughout the rugged panorama of the Himalayas, the fluttering prayer flags, and the colorful thangka art work - a vibrant testament to Buddhism's evolution.

So, as we dive deeper into the wealthy waters of Buddhism, it's essential to don't forget that no matter its extraordinary colleges, the middle stays consistent. The basics have constantly been the same - selling loving-kindness, compassion, knowledge, and peace. This is wherein the beauty of Buddhism lies. Each university is sort of a awesome coloured thread, weaving together a beautiful tapestry that depicts the understanding of Lord Buddha.

11

The Importance of Balance

Have you ever tried taking walks on a tightrope? No? Don't worry, neither have I! The very concept of setting one foot in front of the alternative on a slim, tensioned piece of wire, all whilst swaying precariously above the ground, makes my belly do somersaults. Yet, isn't it interesting how existence frequently looks as if this sensitive balancing act?

Before we dive into the deep sea of facts, permit's get into our metaphorical diving fits and begin with a touch intellectual exercise. Close your eyes for a 2d. Imagine your life is a big scale. On one facet of the size, you've got were given artwork, obligations, and demands; on the other factor, you've got got have been given rest, relaxation, and pleasure. Now, consider it, how balanced is this scale? Is it leaning greater within the course of one component? Are you giving greater weight to paintings and obligations at the price of your nicely-being? Or is it notably balanced?

Did your metaphorical scale sincerely topple over? If so, don't worry. This is wherein the essence of Buddhism sweeps in like a chilled breeze, whispering the secrets and techniques of attaining that elusive stability.

When we communicate of balance in Buddhism, we're now not concerning that nice poise and beauty of a tightrope walker, but to a balance that stems from internal peace, data, and compassion - a stability that permits in reducing pressure, anxiety, and the experience of unease that accompanies an unbalanced lifestyles.

Buddhism taught me the profound truth that stability isn't always a few thing to be attained; it's a few aspect to be placed internal oneself. It's the harmony amongst our thoughts and frame, among our goals and contentment, and most significantly, among our struggles and our peace.

This understanding of balance doesn't are available a single day. It's a method, similar to gaining knowledge of to stroll on a tightrope, except with out the priority of falling! It requires training mindfulness and meditation - the two pillars of Buddhism that assist domesticate focus, beauty, and tranquility.

If you are grappling with the tumultuous waves of existence, preserve in thoughts, it's k if you stumble on the same time as looking for your balance. That's part of the journey. But keep in mind this: being able to stand amidst the chaos with a serene smile, understanding that you have placed your balance, your peace. That's the power of Buddhism. That's the energy of balance.

Balancing Work and Personal Life

Perhaps you find out your self in a similar boat right now, juggling responsibilities and seeking to keep the entirety afloat. But remember, amidst this storm, there may be calm ready to be observed.

Picture this state of affairs: You're on a seesaw, the type you could have loved for your adolescence. On one cease, you've got were given got your paintings — time limits, initiatives, responsibilities. On the opportunity, you have got your non-public life — pursuits, relationships, self-care. The purpose isn't to allow one aspect hit the ground on the equal time as the other soars excessive. The intention is to hold them at equilibrium, suspended in mid-air, playing the view.

So, how are we able to use the training of Buddhism to strike a stability among work and personal lifestyles?

Firstly, permit's begin with mindfulness. Mindfulness, sincerely put, is being definitely gift inside the second. When you're at art work, be at paintings. When you're at home, be at domestic. Avoid thinking about your pending presentation in some unspecified time in the future of your son's soccer suit. Similarly, don't worry about your dishwasher at domestic on the same time as you're in a assembly at artwork. Be fully present anywhere you are. Easier stated than finished, proper? Don't worry; it receives less complex with exercise.

To assist you with this, permit's do a simple workout:

Grab a chunk of paper and a pen.

Draw a line down the center, growing columns. Label one as 'Work' and the alternative as 'Personal.'

In the 'Work' column, listing down all your key art work responsibilities and duties.

In the 'Personal' column, write down the matters that rely maximum to you outdoor of labor, like spending time with circle of relatives, walking in the direction of a hobby, exercise, and so on.

Now, for the following week, consciously attempt to be gift at the same time as doing the duties from every the ones columns.

This exercise will now not satisfactory assist you maintain in thoughts however also visualize how you're dividing some time and electricity.

Secondly, consider to domesticate compassion — for others and, most importantly, for yourself. It's adequate to no longer get the whole lot right all the time. You're now not a robot; you're a superbly complicated guy or girls capable of extraordinary matters however additionally prone to exhaustion. Don't be too hard on yourself. After all, the center of Buddhism teaches us to have loving-kindness closer to all beings, which includes ourselves.

Thirdly, discover time for meditation. Even a few minutes every day may also have a huge impact. It will assist you easy your thoughts, reduce strain, and regain attention. Trust me, it's not 'new age nonsense.' It's a exercise as ancient as time itself and as beneficial as any medication.

Lastly, take shipping of the impermanence of the entirety. Projects will come and flow, closing dates will pass, and your each day to-do listing will sooner or later be cleared. Don't lose your self within the fleeting wishes of hard work and forget about to stay. Remember, life itself is brief.

Remember that quote from Buddha, "Your paintings is to discover your global and then with all of your coronary coronary heart deliver your self to it." Your worldwide isn't entirely composed of hard work. It furthermore consists of you, your family, your passions, and your tranquility. Discover it all, and balance will find out its manner to you.

The Role of Spiritual Practice in Achieving Balance

Picture your existence as a grand orchestra. There are the booming drums of your expert commitments, the shrill violin of societal expectations, the constant rhythm of every day chores, and so on. But wherein's the conductor? Who's making sure that these disparate sounds come collectively to create a symphony and not a cacophony? That's in which spirituality steps in. It is the conductor of your life's orchestra, providing you with the recognize-how to strike a balance.

Chapter 7: Origins Of Buddhism

Buddhism, one of the international's essential religions, has a rich and complicated history that lines its origins lower once more to historical India. This financial ruin delves into the historical context, geographical location, and the existence of its founder, Siddhartha Gautama, who have become referred to as the Buddha. Understanding the origins of Buddhism is essential to apprehend the evolution and development of this influential religious way of life.

2.1 Where did it begin?

Buddhism originated within the northeastern part of the Indian subcontinent, in what is now current-day-day Nepal and northerly India. This vicinity, called the Ganges River Basin, have end up a cradle of civilization and a melting pot of severa cultural and religious traditions throughout the time of the Buddha.

The particular place related to the begin of Buddhism is Lumbini, a small town in gift-day Nepal. It grow to be here that Siddhartha

Gautama, the future Buddha, end up born across the sixth century BCE. Lumbini stays an crucial pilgrimage internet net web page for Buddhists, with the Maya Devi Temple marking the spot in which the Buddha changed into said to had been born.

2.2 When did it start?

The right timeline of the begin and development of Buddhism is a topic of scholarly debate. However, maximum ancient money owed place the beginning of Siddhartha Gautama, the historic parent who may end up the Buddha, at some point of the sixth century BCE. This places the origins of Buddhism in the Axial Age, a length of profound intellectual and spiritual ferment in numerous areas of the place.

Siddhartha Gautama, born proper proper into a royal family, led a sheltered life in the confines of the palace walls. However, as he ventured past the palace grounds, he encountered the realities of antique age, contamination, and loss of lifestyles, which deeply affected him. These encounters sparked his spiritual quest for understanding the person of human struggling and the route to liberation.

2. Three Historical Context

To apprehend the ancient context in which Buddhism emerged, it is important to endure in mind the religious and philosophical landscape of historic India. During the time of the Buddha, India end up domestic to diverse spiritual traditions, together with Hinduism, Jainism, and numerous ascetic and philosophical colleges.

Hinduism, the dominant non secular life-style inside the location, have become characterised with the resource of its complicated pantheon of deities, ritualistic practices, and the caste device. Jainism, based with the resource of the usage of Mahavira, emphasised non-violence and asceticism. Both of those traditions endorsed the cultural and highbrow weather interior which the Buddha's teachings took form.

The social and political milieu of historical India moreover completed a function in shaping Buddhism. The generation changed into marked by means of the rise of urbanization, change networks, and the emergence of new social instructions. The unfold of mind and the quest for spiritual answers had been facilitated by way of improved interactions amongst incredible areas and social companies.

Siddhartha Gautama's selection to surrender his privileged life and are searching out for religious enlightenment modified into a reaction to the societal and existential questions of his time. His teachings offered an possibility direction to salvation and liberation, tough the prevailing religious and social norms.

The historic context wherein Buddhism arose stimulated the language, ideas, and practices located in the Buddhist way of life. As Buddhism advanced and spread in some unspecified time in the future of first-rate regions, it interacted with nearby cultures and absorbed elements from severa philosophical and religious traditions, important to the improvement of numerous Buddhist faculties and sects.

Foundational Teachings

Chapter three explores the essential teachings that form the middle of Buddhism. These teachings provide the framework for information the nature of existence, the motives of suffering, and the course to liberation. The bankruptcy delves into key principles including the Four Noble Truths, the Eightfold Path, and the Three Marks of Existence, that are critical to Buddhist philosophy and workout.

three.1 Fundamental Concepts

At the heart of Buddhism are severa essential ideas that function the building blocks for its teachings. These ideas include impermanence (anicca), non-self (anatta), and suffering (dukkha). Buddhism posits that every one conditioned phenomena are impermanent, continuously converting and trouble to decay. This impermanence extends to the concept of self, tough the belief of a long-lasting and impartial entity.

The concept of struggling, or dukkha, is a pivotal detail in Buddhist teachings. It refers no longer most effective to apparent forms of pain and suffering but also to the unsatisfactoriness and imperfection inherent in all conditioned lifestyles. Buddhism recognizes that struggling is an crucial part of human life and seeks to recognize its motives and alleviate its outcomes.

three.2 Four Noble Truths

The Four Noble Truths form the inspiration of Buddhist philosophy. They define the person of struggling, its motives, the possibility of its cessation, and the path to its cessation. The Four Noble Truths are as follows:

The Truth of Suffering (Dukkha): This reality acknowledges the existence of struggling as an inherent a part of human existence. It encompasses bodily and intellectual pain, dissatisfaction, and the inherent imperfections of life.

The Truth of the Cause of Suffering (Samudaya): This fact identifies yearning and attachment as the foundation motive of struggling. It indicates that attachment to dreams, aversions, and lack of knowledge perpetuates the cycle of suffering.

The Truth of the Cessation of Suffering (Nirodha): This reality offers desire with the useful useful resource of suggesting that the cessation of struggling is plausible. It states that via the cessation of craving and attachment, struggling may be conquer.

The Truth of the Path to the Cessation of Suffering (Magga): This reality outlines the Eightfold Path, which affords steerage on the way to gather liberation from suffering and gain enlightenment.

3.Three Eightfold Path

The Eightfold Path is the realistic guide that ends inside the cessation of struggling and the perception of enlightenment. It encompasses 8 interdependent elements that cover three fundamental areas: expertise, ethical conduct, and highbrow improvement. The Eightfold Path includes the following elements:

Right Understanding: The cultivation of focus and notion into the nature of reality, at the aspect of the understanding of the Four Noble Truths.

Right Intention: The improvement of wholesome intentions and attitudes, collectively with renunciation, compassion, and non-harming.

Right Speech: The practice of honest, kind, and skillful communication, preserving off volatile or divisive speech.

Right Action: Ethical conduct that refrains from harming others, which include abstaining from killing, stealing, and sexual misconduct.

Right Livelihood: Engaging in a livelihood that is ethically sound and does no longer purpose harm to others.

Right Effort: The cultivation of power and dedication in education healthy abilities and leaving in the back of unwholesome ones.

Right Mindfulness: The development of present-2nd recognition and conscious declaration of one's body, emotions, mind, and phenomena.

Right Concentration: The cultivation of centered and collected highbrow states through meditation practices, primary to deep states of interest and insight.

The Eightfold Path provides a comprehensive framework for moral dwelling, highbrow cultivation, and the belief of enlightenment. It serves as a manual for practitioners to enlarge understanding, domesticate virtuous conduct, and cultivate a clean and focused mind.

3. Four Three Marks of Existence

The Three Marks of Existence are essential concepts that light up the man or woman of truth consistent with Buddhist teachings. These marks are impermanence (anicca), struggling (dukkha), and non-self (anatta).

Impermanence (anicca) refers back to the quick and ever-changing nature of all phenomena. Nothing stays constant or eternal, and all conditioned topics are situation to arising and ceasing. Recognizing impermanence allows practitioners permit move of attachments and boom a deeper know-how of the man or woman of reality.

Suffering (dukkha) encompasses the unsatisfactoriness and inherent imperfections of life. It extends past apparent types of pain and consists of the diffused discontentment and dissatisfaction professional in regular life. Understanding the individual of struggling is important to the pursuit of liberation and the cessation of suffering.

Non-self (anatta) demanding situations the idea of a eternal and impartial self. According to Buddhism, there can be no inherent, unchanging self or soul. Instead, the character is visible as a hard and speedy of ever-converting bodily and mental strategies. The recognition of non-self allows practitioners overcome the phantasm of a hard and fast identity and fosters a feel of interconnectedness with all beings.

By thinking of the Three Marks of Existence, practitioners growth insights into the man or woman of fact and gain a deeper information of the motives of struggling. These insights tell the practice of mindfulness, compassion, and the pursuit of liberation from the cycle of suffering.

The Four Noble Truths feature the bedrock of Buddhist philosophy, encapsulating the essence of the Buddha's teachings. They provide a easy assessment of the human situation and offer a roadmap for transcendence. By acknowledging the truth of struggling, practitioners benefit a sensible perspective on the nature of lifestyles, recognizing that struggling is a regular experience that may be understood and triumph over.

The 2nd noble reality, the motive of suffering, sheds moderate on the place of craving and attachment in perpetuating the cycle of dissatisfaction and discontentment. By spotting that desire, clinging, and lack of knowledge are at the basis of struggling, people can domesticate a deeper information in their personal intellectual patterns and artwork inside the route of liberation from the ones causes.

The 1/3 noble reality brings need and reassurance, emphasizing that the cessation of struggling is in reality viable. It holds the promise that via the removal of craving and attachment, people can attain a country of liberation and freedom from struggling. This statistics evokes practitioners to embark on the path of transformation and self-discovery.

The fourth noble fact, the direction to the cessation of suffering, introduces the Eightfold Path due to the fact the manner to accumulate liberation. Each difficulty of the Eightfold Path, from proper records to right interest, represents a vital factor of the spiritual journey. This course offers a holistic approach, integrating expertise, ethics, and intellectual cultivation to guide practitioners in the direction of enlightenment.

The concept of the Three Marks of Existence in addition deepens the statistics of reality in Buddhist teachings. Impermanence (anicca) is a profound perception into the ever-converting nature of phenomena. By spotting the impermanent nature of all subjects, people are endorsed to domesticate non-attachment and encompass the fluidity of existence.

Suffering (dukkha), as the second mark of existence, encompasses no longer nice overt ache and struggling but moreover the subtle forms of discontentment and unsatisfactoriness that pervade human experience. Understanding the all-pervasive nature of suffering permits individuals growth compassion, empathy, and a greater appreciation for the impermanence of pleasure and the futility of chasing external sources of happiness.

Non-self (anatta) demanding conditions the deeply ingrained notion of a set, unbiased self or soul. This coaching invites people to discover the interconnectedness and interdependence of all phenomena. By knowing that there can be no separate, enduring self, humans can permit pass of egoic attachments and domesticate a deeper sense of brotherly love with all beings.

The teachings of the Four Noble Truths, the Eightfold Path, and the Three Marks of Existence art work synergistically, imparting a whole framework for knowledge the person of lifestyles and providing sensible equipment for private transformation. They manual humans on a profound journey of self-discovery, foremost to the notion of enlightenment and the liberation from suffering.

Moreover, those teachings make bigger beyond the theoretical realm, manifesting in everyday lifestyles. Practitioners of Buddhism are advocated to apply these teachings to their thoughts, terms, and movements, cultivating mindfulness, moral conduct, and compassionate attitudes of their interactions with others.

Chapter 8: Requirements And Practices

Chapter four delves into the vital necessities and practices internal Buddhism that facilitates religious growth, moral living, and the cultivation of attention. It explores the ethical hints, meditation and mindfulness practices, monastic life, and the rituals and ceremonies which may be essential to the Buddhist manner of lifestyles.

four.1 Ethical Guidelines

Ethical conduct occupies a relevant feature in Buddhist teachings, supplying a ethical framework for practitioners. The moral hints, regularly referred to as the Five Precepts, are thoughts that guide humans inside the course of compassionate and virtuous conduct. These precepts are:

Refraining from taking life: This precept encourages practitioners to keep away from causing damage to any dwelling being intentionally. It promotes respect for all kinds of existence and the cultivation of non-violence.

Refraining from stealing: The 2d principle urges practitioners to refrain from taking what is not freely given. It emphasizes honesty, integrity, and respect for others' property and belongings.

Refraining from sexual misconduct: This precept encourages practitioners to have interaction in responsible and respectful sexual conduct. It emphasizes constancy, consent, and the avoidance of sexual exploitation or harm.

Refraining from fake speech: Practitioners are advised to be honest and honest in their speech. This principle discourages lying, gossiping, harsh speech, and any shape of speech that motives damage or discord.

Refraining from intoxicants: The final principle advises practitioners to abstain from materials that cloud the thoughts and impair judgment. It promotes clarity, mindfulness, and the cultivation of a balanced and alert united states of america of the united states of thoughts.

By adhering to the ones ethical suggestions, practitioners domesticate a experience of duty, compassion, and mindfulness of their moves, fostering a harmonious and compassionate society.

four.2 Meditation and Mindfulness

Meditation and mindfulness are important practices in Buddhism, serving as powerful tools for self-discovery, recognition, and the cultivation of notion. Various types of meditation are taught and practiced within the Buddhist manner of life, with mindfulness being a prominent thing.

Mindfulness includes cultivating a present-second recognition and non-judgmental observation of one's thoughts, feelings, physical sensations, and the encompassing surroundings. Through mindfulness, practitioners increase an information of the impermanent and conditioned nature of experience, fostering a deeper experience of beauty and equanimity.

Meditation practices variety from interest strategies to insight meditation. Concentration meditation goals to cultivate centered attention and highbrow balance, frequently with the aid of using specializing in a unmarried item including the breath or a specific mantra. Insight meditation, then again, consists of searching on the character of the thoughts and phenomena, cultivating understanding, and growing a right away experiential information of the Three Marks of Existence.

By incorporating meditation and mindfulness practices into their every day lives, practitioners increase readability of thoughts, emotional resilience, and an more potent capability to reply skillfully to lifestyles's annoying situations. These practices additionally deepen self-awareness and cultivate a revel in of interconnectedness and compassion towards oneself and others.

four.Three Monastic Life

Monasticism holds a massive area inner Buddhism, imparting a committed direction for humans to pursue spiritual awakening and the liberation from struggling. Monks (bhikkhus) and nuns (bhikkhunis) renounce worldly attachments and devote themselves to a disciplined and austere life.

Monastic life includes strict adherence to moral guidelines, intensive meditation exercise, and the have a take a look at and safety of Buddhist teachings. Monastics live in monasteries or nunneries, forming a community (Sangha) that facilitates their non secular boom and serves as a custodian of the Buddhist way of life.

The monastic route gives an surroundings conducive to focused exercise, loose from worldly distractions. Monastics give up cloth possessions, adopt a smooth and ascetic life-style, and depend upon the generosity of laypractitioners for his or her critical goals. This reliance on alms and the help of the lay network fosters a symbiotic dating amongst monastics and laypeople, with each playing a crucial position in assisting the opportunity's spiritual adventure.

Monastic life offers a platform for deepening meditation exercise, reading Buddhist scriptures, and attractive in communal rituals and ceremonies. Monastics devote themselves to the pursuit of interest, compassion, and the conclusion of enlightenment, serving as religious courses and exemplars for lay practitioners.

While monastic existence isn't always a demand for all Buddhists, it serves as an concept and reminder of the ideals and commitments good sized to the Buddhist course. Lay practitioners, at the same time as engaged in their regular lives, try to stay in accordance with the ethical thoughts, interact in regular meditation exercise, and manual the monastic community through offerings and acts of generosity.

4. Four Rituals and Ceremonies

Rituals and ceremonies play an essential function in the Buddhist way of lifestyles, offering opportunities for communal worship, expression of devotion, and the transmission of teachings. These rituals and ceremonies range for the duration of specific Buddhist traditions and cultures however frequently contain the chanting of scriptures, prostrations, presenting of plants, incense, and candles, and the recitation of prayers or mantras.

Rituals and ceremonies feature a way to cultivate mindfulness, gratitude, and reverence, deepening the religious connection with the training and the network. They offer a experience of continuity with the historical lineage of Buddhism and function crucial events for celebrating big events within the existence of the Buddha and different respected figures.

One enormous ritual in Buddhism is the act of taking safe haven within the Triple Gem or Three Jewels – the Buddha (the awoke one), the Dharma (the commands), and the Sangha (the network of practitioners). Taking shelter indicates a commitment to observe the Buddhist path and are looking for guidance and help from the Three Jewels.

While rituals and ceremonies preserve cultural and traditional importance, their essence lies in the intention, devotion, and internal transformation they inspire. They offer a method for human beings to specific their religious aspirations, deepen their connection to the training, and foster a revel in of team spirit within the Buddhist community.

Ethical recommendations function a compass for ethical conduct, guiding human beings to behave with kindness, compassion, and integrity. By adhering to the Five Precepts, practitioners expand a heightened experience of obligation towards themselves and others. This dedication to ethical residing fosters harmonious relationships, social concord, and the cultivation of a virtuous individual.

The practices of meditation and mindfulness provide practitioners a path to internal peace, self-discovery, and the improvement of notion. Through ordinary meditation workout, human beings learn how to calm the thoughts, cultivate readability, and gain a deeper information of the nature of their thoughts, emotions, and opinions. Mindfulness, every on and stale the meditation cushion, complements present-second interest, allowing practitioners to fully have interaction with the richness of existence and growth a extra profound revel in of popularity and equanimity.

Monastic existence, at the equal time as now not pursued thru all Buddhists, exemplifies the committed pursuit of non secular awakening and the renunciation of worldly attachments. The monastic path gives an surroundings conducive to deepening exercising and characteristic a study, fostering a experience of region, simplicity, and detachment from cloth possessions. Monastics characteristic beacons of concept, reminding lay practitioners of the possibilities of a committed non secular life and presenting guidance on the path to liberation.

Rituals and ceremonies preserve a completely particular vicinity in Buddhism, serving as sacred sports for the community to return again again together and unique devotion. These rituals provide a experience of connection to the historical lineage of Buddhism and create a area for human beings to reflect, ponder, and deepen their non secular connection. Through participation in rituals, practitioners domesticate a enjoy of reverence, gratitude, and interconnectedness, enriching their non secular lives and strengthening their connection to the wider Buddhist network.

The requirements and practices inside Buddhism are not isolated elements but an interconnected tapestry that enables and reinforces each distinctive. Ethical conduct lays the muse for the development of mindfulness and attention, enabling practitioners to engage in deeper meditation and advantage insights into the individual of reality. Monastic lifestyles exemplifies the devoted pursuit of religious boom and serves as an thought for lay practitioners to deepen their dedication to the Buddhist path. Rituals and ceremonies provide a technique for human beings to unique their devotion, foster network cohesion, and nourish the non secular length in their lives.

Ultimately, the necessities and practices in Buddhism aren't mere rituals or obligations but system for non-public transformation and non secular awakening. They provide a roadmap for people to navigate the complexities of human lifestyles, cultivate inner peace, and boom understanding and compassion. By carrying out those practices, practitioners now not best benefit themselves but moreover contribute to the well-being and harmony of society as a whole.

Chapter 9: Beliefs And Philosophy

Chapter five delves into the center ideals and philosophical underpinnings of Buddhism. It explores necessities which include karma, rebirth, established origination, and the closing intention of enlightenment. Understanding the beliefs and philosophy of Buddhism is vital to comprehending the worldview and guiding necessities of this historical manner of lifestyles.

5.1 Karma and Rebirth

Karma and rebirth are critical ideas in Buddhism that shed slight on the nature of motive and impact and the continuity of life beyond a unmarried lifetime. According to Buddhist teachings, karma refers to the intentional moves of frame, speech, and mind that form an person's destiny research. Positive moves bring about remarkable results, while poor moves bring about terrible consequences.

The concept of rebirth, or reincarnation, asserts that recognition continues to show up in new our our bodies after the dying of the physical frame. Rebirth is not seen as a continuation of an unchanging self or soul however as an possibility because the continuity of attention stimulated by means of manner of past moves (karma). The cycle of rebirth maintains until liberation from the cycle of struggling is attained.

The information of karma and rebirth encourages practitioners to take obligation for their actions, as they apprehend that their gift instances are stimulated through beyond moves and that their destiny studies depend upon their modern alternatives. It offers a framework for facts the ethical implications of 1's actions and fosters a feel of personal corporation agency and duty.

5.2 Dependent Origination

Dependent origination, additionally known as interdependent bobbing up, is a crucial idea in Buddhist philosophy that elucidates the interconnected nature of all phenomena. It explains how all subjects rise up and exist in dependence on multiple motives and conditions, as an alternative of getting an inherent and unbiased life.

According to based origination, the whole lot within the worldwide is interconnected and arises because of a web of interdependent reasons and conditions. This understanding dismantles the phantasm of a separate and glued self, because it exhibits that one's mind, feelings, and opinions are inspired thru manner of a complicated network of things.

The doctrine of based origination is frequently depicted thru the twelve hyperlinks of installed origination, which illustrate the cycle of existence and the motives of suffering. This framework allows individuals understand the reasons and situations that provide upward push to struggling and offers notion into the route to liberation from this cycle.

By understanding hooked up origination, practitioners amplify a deeper experience of interconnectedness, compassion, and non-attachment. They apprehend that their movements and picks have a long way-carrying out consequences, no longer high-quality for themselves however moreover for the well-being of others and the area at massive.

five.Three The Ultimate Goal: Enlightenment

The last purpose of Buddhism is the attainment of enlightenment, moreover known as Nirvana or Awakening. Enlightenment is the dominion of whole liberation from suffering, lack of statistics, and the cycle of begin and lack of life. It is the perception of the right nature of truth and the cessation of all intellectual defilements.

Enlightenment is characterised via the use of the direct experiential understanding of the Four Noble Truths, the Three Marks of Existence, and the individual of based totally completely origination. It brings approximately profound cognizance, compassion, and freedom from all types of craving and attachment.

While enlightenment is regularly depicted as an person attainment, Buddhism emphasizes the interconnectedness of all beings. The aspiration for enlightenment extends past personal liberation and includes the purpose to help others at the route of awakening.

The course to enlightenment is multifaceted and can variety amongst one-of-a-kind Buddhist traditions. It consists of the cultivation of consciousness through have a study, contemplation, and meditation, in addition to the development of compassion, ethical conduct, and the eradication of defilements.

Attaining enlightenment is taken into consideration a unprecedented and tough employer, requiring dedicated exercising, perseverance, and the steering of certified teachers. However, Buddhism moreover acknowledges that development can be made at each degree of the path, or even small steps toward enlightenment bring about extremely good transformation and liberation from suffering.

The pursuit of enlightenment serves as a guiding principle for Buddhist practitioners, inspiring them to broaden knowledge, cultivate compassion, and stay in alignment with the training. While the final cause may additionally seem remote, the journey itself is transformative, bringing about greater peace, readability, and a profound information of the individual of fact.

5.Four Diversity and Interpretations

It is vital to word that Buddhism includes a wealthy form of interpretations and practices, inspired with the useful resource of severa cultural, ancient, and geographical contexts. Different Buddhist traditions also can location varying emphasis on positive ideals and philosophical concepts, and their interpretations of karma, rebirth, based totally origination, and enlightenment can variety.

For instance, in Theravada Buddhism, practiced in maximum instances in Southeast Asia, there is a robust emphasis on individual liberation and the monastic path. Mahayana Buddhism, famous in East Asia, emphasizes the cultivation of compassion and the aspiration to gain enlightenment now not only for oneself however furthermore for the advantage of all sentient beings. Vajrayana Buddhism, determined particularly in Tibet and the Himalayan regions, consists of esoteric practices and rituals to expedite the route to enlightenment.

The kind of interpretations inner Buddhism permits for a richness and adaptableness that allows the life-style to resonate with people from remarkable cultures and backgrounds. It highlights the dynamic nature of Buddhism and its capacity to conform and adapt to changing instances and contexts.

Chapter 10: Buddhism Within The Modern World

Chapter 6 explores the version and transformation of Buddhism within the cutting-edge world. It examines how Buddhism has spread beyond its traditional cultural limitations, the effect of globalization on the Buddhist tradition, and the annoying conditions and opportunities supplied in contemporary-day society. This bankruptcy sheds mild at the methods in which Buddhism has evolved and maintains to resonate with people in the 21st century.

6.1 Global Spread of Buddhism

Buddhism, to start with rooted in ancient India, has extended an prolonged way beyond its conventional cultural limitations. The teachings of the Buddha have traversed continents, spreading all through Asia and conducting the beaches of Europe, North America, and different components of the area. Today, Buddhism is a worldwide faith with thousands and lots of adherents for the duration of severa cultures and societies.

The unfold of Buddhism has been facilitated thru different factors, which encompass migration, change, missionary efforts, and the dissemination of Buddhist texts and teachings. As human beings from outstanding backgrounds and cultures encountered Buddhism, they interpreted and assimilated its teachings in strategies that resonated with their very own worldviews and cultural contexts. This has brought about the emergence of remarkable Buddhist traditions and faculties, every with its unique practices and interpretations.

6.2 Impact of Globalization

Globalization, with its interconnectedness and change of thoughts, has had a great effect on Buddhism. Increased tour, communique, and the provision of statistics have facilitated the dissemination of Buddhist teachings and practices in the course of the globe. This has allowed humans from numerous backgrounds to get right of entry to Buddhist teachings and have interaction in Buddhist practices, even in regions wherein Buddhism has traditionally been absent.

Furthermore, globalization has supplied opportunities for pass-cultural communicate and the trade of thoughts between Buddhist practitioners and pupils from notable traditions. This has brought on a deepening understanding of the diverse interpretations and practices internal Buddhism, fostering mutual recognize and collaboration.

At the same time, globalization has moreover furnished worrying situations to traditional Buddhist practices and values. The speedy pace of modern-day existence, consumerism, and materialistic interests can create limitations to the cultivation of mindfulness, ethical living, and the pursuit of spiritual boom. Additionally, the have an effect on of secularism and skepticism in a few societies has posed worrying conditions to the conventional spiritual framework of Buddhism.

6. Three Engaged Buddhism

Engaged Buddhism is a motion that emerged within the twentieth century, emphasizing the lively involvement of Buddhists in social, political, and environmental troubles. Engaged Buddhists looking for to use the ideas and values of Buddhism to address societal problems and sell best change in the worldwide.

Engaged Buddhism encompasses severa forms of social activism, which encompass human rights advocacy, environmental conservation, peacebuilding, and community development. By actively collaborating within the ones areas, Engaged Buddhists purpose to alleviate suffering, sell compassion, and cultivate a greater just and equitable society.

This movement has obtained traction in plenty of components of the world, specifically in response to social injustices, environmental crises, and conflicts. Engaged Buddhists apprehend the interconnectedness of all beings and the responsibility to art work in the path of the welfare and liberation of all.

6. Four Buddhism and Science

In cutting-edge years, Buddhism and generation have engaged in a fruitful speak, with scholars and scientists exploring the intersection of these disciplines. This communicate has induced collaborations, research duties, and conferences, examining areas including the neuroscience of meditation, the psychology of mindfulness, and the exploration of cognizance.

The compatibility amongst Buddhism and era arises from their shared emphasis on empirical observation, crucial inquiry, and the search for know-how the man or woman of truth. Buddhist practices, collectively with meditation and mindfulness, had been subjects of medical research, presenting treasured insights into highbrow well-being, attentional strategies, and the neuroscience of attention.

The speak among Buddhism and technology has now not most effective deepened our statistics of the thoughts and human experience but has additionally contributed to the broader communicate at the man or woman of fact, reputation, and the interconnectednessof all phenomena. It highlights the capability for complementary perspectives from both disciplines, presenting new avenues for exploration and a extra holistic information of the human experience.

6. Five Challenges and Opportunities

While Buddhism has located a global presence and keeps to inspire and guide people, it also faces demanding situations in the cutting-edge-day global. The fast pace of life, materialistic values, and the dominance of technology can create distractions and preclude the cultivation of mindfulness and non secular increase.

Moreover, as Buddhism encounters new cultural contexts, it must adapt and reply to the needs and issues of modern-day society. This calls for locating approaches to talk the schooling efficiently, addressing social and environmental troubles, and attractive with numerous corporations.

However, the modern worldwide additionally gives possibilities for Buddhism to thrive. The availability of technology and virtual structures lets in broader get proper of entry to to Buddhist teachings and practices, conducting folks who may not have had get right of access to to them previously. Online groups, meditation apps, and digital teachings have extended the reach of Buddhism, fostering connections and useful resource networks for the duration of the globe.

Furthermore, the growing hobby in mindfulness, meditation, and holistic well-being offers an possibility for Buddhism to make contributions to the discourse on intellectual fitness, pressure good buy, and general properly-being. Buddhist teachings and practices provide precious equipment for people to navigate the disturbing situations of contemporary-day life, cultivate inner peace, and broaden more resilience.

Chapter 11: Interfaith Dialogue And Buddhism

Chapter 7 explores the placement of Buddhism in interfaith talk, emphasizing the significance of mutual records, respect, and collaboration amongst one-of-a-kind spiritual traditions. It delves into the thoughts and practices that manual interfaith talk and highlights the contributions of Buddhism to fostering harmonious relationships and promoting spiritual pluralism.

7.1 Principles of Interfaith Dialogue

Interfaith communicate is a way of accomplishing enormous conversations and exchanges amongst representatives of numerous spiritual traditions. It is primarily based at the standards of mutual apprehend, expertise, and the recognition of the shared values and aspirations amongst numerous non secular groups.

In interfaith speak, people are seeking out to construct bridges of communication, dispel misconceptions, and sell peaceful coexistence. The ideas of energetic listening, empathy, and the popularity of the intrinsic really worth and dignity of absolutely everyone manual the way of interfaith speak.

The purpose of interfaith speak is not to merge or homogenize spiritual traditions but as an alternative to understand and have an first-rate time their unique contributions to the richness of human enjoy. Through communicate, contributors have a look at from each specific, deepen their very personal faith perspectives, and find common floor for collaboration in addressing societal demanding situations.

7.2 Buddhist Contributions to Interfaith Dialogue

Buddhism brings severa unique contributions to interfaith communicate. Its middle teachings, collectively with compassion, non-violence, and the recognition of the interdependence of all beings, provide a basis for speak based totally on expertise and harmony.

Buddhism's emphasis on mindfulness and self-reflected picture encourages practitioners to domesticate openness, hobby, and deep listening—the important functions for fruitful interfaith communicate. The workout of mindfulness permits people to be fully present, to stoop judgment, and to have interaction with others in a compassionate and non-confrontational way.

Buddhism furthermore gives a philosophical framework that enhances interfaith communicate. Concepts which encompass vacancy (sunyata) and the Middle Way offer insights into the individual of truth and the possibility of embracing variety without clinging to consistent perspectives. These teachings foster humility, openness, and a willingness to look at from terrific views.

Moreover, Buddhist history is replete with examples of interfaith engagement. Throughout the centuries, Buddhists have interacted with practitioners of various faiths, assignment philosophical discussions, modern collaborations, and the alternate of thoughts. These interactions have contributed to the enrichment and evolution of Buddhist idea and exercise.

7. Three Challenges and Opportunities in Interfaith Dialogue

Interfaith talk isn't with out its annoying conditions. Cultural variations, theological disagreements, and ancient tensions can create boundaries to records and collaboration. However, these annoying situations moreover gift opportunities for growth, as they invite individuals to interact in deep listening, empathy, and a willingness to discover common ground.

One assignment is the potential for misrepresentation or false impression of Buddhist teachings and practices. It is critical for people in interfaith communicate to technique Buddhism with an correct records, recognizing its diverse interpretations and practices throughout tremendous cultural contexts.

Another challenge is the want to address social and moral issues that intersect with religious beliefs. Buddhism can make contributions to interfaith speak by using sharing its insights on compassion, social justice, and environmental stewardship. By addressing the ones problems together, spiritual businesses can work inside the route of a greater just and sustainable international.

The possibilities in interfaith speak are high-quality. It gives a platform for spiritual communities to unite in addressing global annoying conditions, together with poverty, inequality, and climate trade. Through collaboration, shared values, and collective movement, non secular traditions, collectively with Buddhism, could have a big wonderful effect on the arena.

Interfaith speak moreover fosters private boom, as people encounter diverse perspectives and have interaction in self-reflection. It broadens one's records of numerous non secular traditions, deepens one's appreciation for the complexity of human spirituality, and promotes a extra inclusive and empathetic worldview.

Chapter 12: Buddhism And Ethics

Chapter 8 delves into the ethical dimensions of Buddhism, exploring the ideas, values, and practices that manual ethical conduct in the Buddhist life-style. It examines the significance of ethics inside the pursuit of non secular increase and liberation from suffering, and the way Buddhist ethics extends beyond individual behavior to encompass social and environmental obligation.

8.1 The Foundation of Buddhist Ethics

Ethical behavior, called sila, bureaucracy the foundation of Buddhist workout. Sila encompasses the requirements and recommendations that guide people in their mind, speech, and movements. It emphasizes the cultivation of virtues which encompass compassion, honesty, generosity, and mindfulness.

The ethical framework in Buddhism is grounded inside the understanding of karma—the law of cause and effect. The idea of karma highlights the interplay between movements and their results, emphasizing the importance of acting with aim and recognition.

The Five Precepts, which have been noted in advance, characteristic essential recommendations for ethical conduct in Buddhism. They offer a framework for practitioners to refrain from harming others, have interaction in honest and respectful communication, domesticate sexual responsibility, exercising truthfulness, and avoid intoxicants that cloud the thoughts.

8.2 Ethical Conduct and Spiritual Growth

Ethical behavior isn't always appeared as a set of tips imposed from outside belongings however as a way for personal increase and the cultivation of information. It is visible as an crucial part of the religious route, helping the improvement of mindfulness, attention, and perception.

Engaging in moral conduct purifies the thoughts, developing the situations crucial for the cultivation of knowledge and the realization of enlightenment. By appearing in alignment with moral ideas, human beings reduce the motives of struggling, expand first-rate intellectual states, and domesticate a revel in of inner concord.

Ethical behavior also enhances interpersonal relationships, fostering take delivery of as genuine with, recognize, and harmonious coexistence. By cultivating virtues which includes compassion and generosity, people contribute to the welfare of others, developing a first-rate ripple impact in their immediate surroundings and society at big.

8.Three Social and Environmental Responsibility

Buddhist ethics extends past individual behavior to embody social and environmental obligation. Buddhism acknowledges the interconnectedness of all beings and emphasizes the importance of working in the path of the welfare and liberation of all.

In the social sphere, Buddhist teachings emphasize requirements which consist of social justice, equality, and compassion for all beings. Buddhism encourages humans to have interaction in acts of service, alleviate the struggling of others, and sell fairness and equity in society.

Environmental duty is likewise integral to Buddhist ethics. Buddhism emphasizes the interdependence among human beings and the natural worldwide, spotting the importance of ecological stability for the nicely-being of all beings. Buddhist teachings advise for sustainable dwelling, the conservation of natural resources, and the good buy of damage to the surroundings.

eight.Four Ethical Challenges inside the Modern World

In the contemporary-day worldwide, Buddhist ethics face severa stressful situations. The globalized and consumerist way of existence, pushed with the aid of manner of manner of materialistic values, can sell selfishness, greed, and environmental degradation. Additionally, upgrades in generation enhance new moral dilemmas and questions, which encompass the ethical use of artificial intelligence and the accountable manage of digital information.

However, Buddhist ethics additionally offer steerage and answers to the ones traumatic conditions. The cultivation of mindfulness and ethical reputation permits humans navigate the complexities of the modern-day-day global and make alternatives which are regular with their values and the properly-being of others.

Moreover, Buddhist teachings promote a shift in interest—a float faraway from a self-targeted mindset closer to an data of interconnectedness and the cultivation of compassion. This shift in focus can inspire humans and companies to deal with societal and environmental issues and artwork inside the route of a extra certainly and sustainable worldwide.

8. Five Engaged Buddhism and Social Activism

Engaged Buddhism, as noted in advance, highlights the lively involvement of Buddhists in addressing social, political, and environmental issues. Engaged Buddhists comply with Buddhist requirements and values to promote fantastic change in societyand advocate for social justice, peace, and environmental sustainability.

Engaged Buddhists have interaction in severa styles of social activism, collectively with advocating for human rights, running in the direction of poverty remedy, selling non-violence, and addressing environmental issues. They understand the interconnectedness of all beings and the interaction amongst person actions and societal properly-being.

Engaged Buddhism demonstrates that ethical behavior isn't always confined to personal conduct but extends to collective motion and social transformation. It emphasizes the importance of translating Buddhist thoughts into tangible efforts that deal with systemic injustices and sell the welfare of all beings.

Chapter 13: Buddhism And Mindfulness

Chapter nine explores the profound dating amongst Buddhism and mindfulness. It delves into the origins and development of mindfulness inside the Buddhist way of existence, its transformative power, and its current-day programs in severa elements of life.

nine.1 The Origins of Mindfulness in Buddhism

Mindfulness, called sati in Pali and smriti in Sanskrit, has its roots inside the teachings of the Buddha. It is one of the critical elements of the Noble Eightfold Path—the direction to the cessation of struggling and the belief of enlightenment.

The Buddha emphasised the cultivation of mindfulness as a way to extend belief and overcome the highbrow defilements that cause suffering. Mindfulness includes being absolutely gift, observing the man or woman of one's mind, emotions, bodily sensations, and the surrounding environment without judgment or attachment.

In Buddhist workout, mindfulness is cultivated thru numerous techniques, which encompass formal meditation, each day sports activities, and the exercising of mindfulness in every day life. The goal is to boom a 2nd-to-2d hobby that permits for a direct and easy records of the impermanent and conditioned nature of all reminiscences.

9.2 The Transformative Power of Mindfulness

Mindfulness is legitimate for its transformative power within the Buddhist manner of existence. By cultivating mindfulness, human beings boom a deep information of the workings of the thoughts and the character of suffering. It lets in for the direct remark of thoughts, emotions, and sensations, allowing practitioners to cultivate clarity, equanimity, and focus.

Through mindfulness, humans end up privy to the steady fluctuations in their highbrow states and the recurring forms of the mind. This attention offers an opportunity to recognize and allow skip of unwholesome mind and feelings, fostering a revel in of freedom and internal peace.

Mindfulness moreover complements the functionality to reply skillfully to life's disturbing situations and cultivate immoderate first rate highbrow states which encompass compassion, loving-kindness, and gratitude. By being in reality observed in each 2d, people can have interaction with life extra authentically and increase a deeper connection to themselves and others.

nine.Three Mindfulness in Contemporary Contexts

In modern some years, mindfulness has acquired enormous interest and recognition beyond the boundaries of the Buddhist life-style. Its programs have advanced into various secular contexts, which include healthcare, psychology, schooling, and the workplace.

Mindfulness-primarily based interventions were advanced to deal with more than a few issues, at the side of stress cut price, pain control, tension, melancholy, and addiction. The workout of mindfulness has established promising consequences in enhancing regular properly-being, enhancing mental fitness, and promoting resilience.

In healthcare settings, mindfulness is blanketed into treatments which includes Mindfulness-Based Stress Reduction (MBSR) and Mindfulness-Based Cognitive Therapy (MBCT). These strategies appoint mindfulness practices to cultivate self-popularity, lessen misery, and promote recuperation and self-care.

In training, mindfulness programs are being completed to foster emotional law, attentional capabilities, and social-emotional studying among college college students. Mindfulness practices offer gear for kids and kids to manipulate pressure, decorate recognition, and increase empathy and compassion.

Furthermore, mindfulness is being incorporated into administrative center settings to beautify employee nicely-being, lessen stress, and enhance productivity. Mindfulness-primarily based programs in agencies provide strategies to domesticate resilience, conversation talents, and emotional intelligence.

9.4 Mindfulness and Ethics

In the Buddhist life-style, mindfulness is inseparable from ethical conduct. The cultivation of mindfulness is in element associated with the improvement of virtues collectively with compassion, non-harming, and moral popularity.

Mindfulness allows people to have a look at their intentions and movements, cultivating an extended sensitivity to the impact of their alternatives on themselves and others. It fosters a deep experience of obligation and encourages the improvement of ethical conduct and compassionate movement.

By cultivating mindfulness, people come to be more attuned to their moral values and act in alignment with them. Mindfulness exercise supports the popularity of the interconnectedness of all beings andencourages ethical conduct that promotes the welfare and liberation of all.

9.Five Mindfulness as a Spiritual Practice

While mindfulness has determined huge secular applications, it remains an vital a part of the Buddhist non secular path. Mindfulness workout is not in reality centered on strain discount or improved ordinary performance but is deeply intertwined with the pursuit of liberation from struggling and the realization of enlightenment.

Within the Buddhist context, mindfulness is practiced as a part of a whole path that consists of ethical conduct, meditation, statistics cultivation, and the improvement of compassion. Mindfulness serves as a basis for deepening awareness, investigating the character of fact, and developing perception into the impermanence, unsatisfactoriness, and selflessness of all phenomena.

The exercise of mindfulness allows the development of abilties which includes equanimity, non-attachment, and an embodied presence that permits for a right away revel in of the winning 2d. It is through this direct revel in that practitioners benefit profound insights into the person of suffering and the capability for liberation.

9.6 Mindfulness and the Path to Awakening

In Buddhism, mindfulness isn't always regarded as a purpose in itself however as a manner to cultivate the elements critical for religious awakening. The exercising of mindfulness enables the development of cognizance (samadhi), which sooner or later finally ends up within the deepening of perception (vipassana).

By cultivating mindfulness, human beings broaden a heightened interest of the springing up and passing of intellectual and bodily phenomena, predominant to the notion of their impermanent and conditioned nature. This notion into the character of fact allows the liberation from clinging, attachment, and the motives of struggling.

The exercise of mindfulness furthermore nurtures the development of information, compassion, and the cultivation of healthful highbrow states. As practitioners deepen their mindfulness exercise, they grow to be more attuned to the interconnectedness of all beings, cultivating a feel of care, empathy, and an aspiration to alleviate struggling in themselves and others.

Chapter 14: Buddhism And The Path To Liberation

Chapter 10 delves into the middle teachings and practices of Buddhism that lead to liberation from suffering and the belief of enlightenment. It explores the route to liberation, the region of meditation and knowledge, and the transformative journey in the direction of non secular awakening.

10.1 The Four Noble Truths

At the heart of Buddhism are the Four Noble Truths, which offer the framework for facts the person of suffering and the route to liberation. The Four Noble Truths are:

The Truth of Suffering (Dukkha): The reputation that lifestyles is inherently marked thru suffering, dissatisfaction, and impermanence. Suffering arises from attachment, aversion, and lack of knowledge.

The Truth of the Origin of Suffering (Samudaya): The understanding that suffering arises from yearning and clinging, fueled via using lack of statistics of the real nature of fact. Craving and clinging create a cycle of dissatisfaction and perpetuate the cycle of rebirth.

The Truth of the Cessation of Suffering (Nirodha): The reputation that the cessation of suffering is possible through the usage of removing craving and clinging, due to this engaging in liberation from the cycle of transport and dying.

The Truth of the Path to the Cessation of Suffering (Magga): The reputation that there can be a course, called the Noble Eightfold Path, that outcomes inside the cessation of struggling and the conclusion of enlightenment.

10.2 The Noble Eightfold Path

The Noble Eightfold Path, as elucidated with the beneficial aid of the Buddha, is the path to liberation and the conclusion of enlightenment. It consists of 8 interconnected elements that guide practitioners in cultivating understanding, moral behavior, and highbrow development. The Noble Eightfold Path includes:

Right View: The correct records of the character of truth, the Four Noble Truths, and the law of karma.

Right Intention: The cultivation of wholesome intentions and the renunciation of harmful thoughts, dreams, and motivations.

Right Speech: The exercising of honest, type, and skillful communication, averting dangerous speech together with lying, divisive speech, harsh speech, and gossip.

Right Action: The cultivation of moral conduct, refraining from harming residing beings, stealing, carrying out sexual misconduct, and working towards generosity and compassion.

Right Livelihood: Engaging in an career that is honorable, ethical, and supports the nicely-being of others, maintaining off livelihoods that contain damage, deception, or exploitation.

Right Effort: The cultivation of diligent try and wilderness unwholesome highbrow states, cultivate healthful highbrow states, and preserve a balanced and focused thoughts.

Right Mindfulness: The cultivation of present-2d reputation and mindfulness in all sports activities, looking the frame, emotions, thoughts, and phenomena with clarity and equanimity.

Right Concentration: The development of centered, calm, and centered states of mind thru meditation exercising, leading to deep states of absorption (jhana) and the direct attention of the man or woman of reality.

The Noble Eightfold Path is not a linear development but a holistic and integrated technique to non secular improvement. The elements of the route guide and supply a boost to every special, principal to the cultivation of understanding, moral behavior, and highbrow purification.

10.3 Meditation and Mental Development

Meditation is a important practice inner Buddhism, serving as a method to increase attention, mindfulness, and notion. It gives a direct experiential exploration of the mind and facilitates the cultivation of knowledge and the cessation of struggling.

The exercise of meditation encompasses severa techniques, at the side of mindfulness of breath (anapanasati), loving-kindness (metta), compassion (karuna), and perception meditation (vipassana). These practices contain the cultivation of gift-second consciousness, the improvement of attention, and the research of the character of thoughts and phenomena.

Through meditation, practitioners increase the capability to take a look at the bobbing up and passing of thoughts, feelings, and sensations with out attachment or aversion.

This cultivates a deep understanding of the impermanent, unsatisfactory, and selfless nature of all phenomena, leading to insights into the character of fact and the cessation of suffering.

Meditation furthermore promotes the development of effective intellectual states together with compassion, loving-kindness, and equanimity. It allows people domesticate a experience of inner peace, resilience, and a compassionate mind-set closer to themselves and others.

10.Four The Role of Wisdom and Insight

Wisdom, called prajna in Buddhism, is a critical element of the direction to liberation. It entails the direct interest and knowledge of the genuine nature of reality, transcending traditional notions of self and the delusions of ego.

Wisdom arises from the cultivation of mindfulness, research, and contemplation of the character of mind and phenomena. It lets in people to apprehend the impermanent, unsatisfactory, and selfless nature of all conditioned phenomena, main to a profound shift in belief and information.

Insight (vipassana) meditation plays a important role in developing know-how. Through the practice of insight meditation, people check out the arising and passing of testimonies, looking at the three traits of lifestyles—impermanence (anicca), unsatisfactoriness (dukkha), and non-self (anatta).

Insight meditation allows practitioners to penetrate the illusions of the ego, to appearance through the delusions of attachment and aversion, and to expand a proper away know-how of the interconnectedness and interdependence of all phenomena. This notion ends inside the stop of the emptiness (sunyata) of inherent existence and the liberation from struggling.

10.5 The Transformative Journey

The path to liberation inside Buddhism isn't a short restore or an outdoor attainment but a transformative adventure of self-discovery and internal cultivation. It calls for dedication, perseverance, and a willingness to confront the deep-seated kinds of attachment, aversion, and lack of know-how.

The transformative journey closer to liberation is characterized thru the cultivation of mindfulness, moral behavior, highbrow improvement, and the deepening of knowledge and notion. It consists of the purification of the mind, the gradual eradication of defilements, and the perception of the actual nature of truth.

This adventure is not restricted to monastic practitioners but is open to people from all walks of existence. It is a course of personal transformation that may be incorporated into one's each day lifestyles, relationships, and engagement with the world.

10.6 Liberation and the Attainment of Enlightenment

The final intention of the Buddhist path is liberation from struggling and the notion of enlightenment—moreover known as Nirvana or Awakening. Enlightenment is the direct experiential attention of the Four Noble Truths and the cessation of all highbrow defilements.

Enlightenment brings approximately profound cognizance, compassion, and freedom from all varieties of craving and attachment. It is characterized thru way of the direct awareness of the right nature of fact and the transcendence of traditional notions of self.

While the attainment of enlightenment can be uncommon and require devoted exercise, Buddhism acknowledges that improvement may be made at every degree of the path. Even small steps closer to liberation result in extremely good transformation and contribute to the cessation of suffering.

Chapter 15: Buddhist Practices And Rituals

Chapter eleven explores the numerous fashions of practices and rituals in the Buddhist way of existence. It examines the characteristic of rituals in expressing devotion, cultivating mindfulness, and fostering a experience of network. The economic catastrophe additionally delves into the significance of key practices consisting of meditation, chanting, and pilgrimage.

eleven.1 The Role of Rituals in Buddhism

Rituals maintain an essential place in Buddhism, serving as way to express devotion, reverence, and gratitude in the direction of the Buddha, Dharma (the lessons), and Sangha (the community of practitioners). Rituals provide a tangible way to connect to the spiritual dimensions of Buddhism and evoke a sense of sacredness.

Rituals in Buddhism frequently consist of symbolic gestures, chants, offerings, and the use of ritual objects. They can take place in temples, monasteries, or in the homes of practitioners. Through rituals, practitioners have interaction their senses, cultivating mindfulness and growing a conducive surroundings for spiritual exercising.

While rituals vary at some point of unique Buddhist traditions and cultures, their underlying cause is to deepen one's connection to the lessons and the spiritual path. Rituals can also serve as a manner to mark crucial lifestyles sports, which encompass delivery, marriage, and death, supplying solace and steerage in the course of massive transitions.

eleven.2 Meditation as a Central Practice

Meditation holds a brilliant area in Buddhist exercising, serving as a transformative tool for cultivating mindfulness, attention, and insight. It is thru meditation that practitioners develop a deep information of the mind, the man or woman of reality, and the cessation of suffering.

Various meditation strategies are practiced within Buddhism, along side mindfulness of breath (anapanasati), loving-kindness (metta), belief (vipassana), and visualization. These practices involve the cultivation of present-2nd interest, the improvement of interest, and the studies of the man or woman of thoughts and phenomena.

Meditation permits practitioners to check the arising and passing of thoughts, emotions, and sensations, cultivating a deep experience of perception into the impermanence, unsatisfactoriness, and selflessness of all conditioned phenomena. Through sustained workout, meditation ends in the deepening of know-how and the perception of the individual of fact.

11. Three Chanting and Recitation

Chanting and recitation of Buddhist texts and mantras are conventional practices in lots of Buddhist traditions. Chanting serves multiple capabilities, together with invoking benefits, expressing devotion, and cultivating mindfulness.

Chanting may be accomplished for my part or together, frequently discovered through manner of using the rhythmic beating of drums, the ringing of bells, or the use of musical gadgets. Through the repetition of sacred phrases and terms, practitioners attention their minds, immerse themselves inside the teachings, and create an surroundings of reverence.

Chanting moreover serves as a form of oral transmission, keeping and passing down the training from era to era. The melodic and rhythmic excellent of chants can create a revel in of concord, fostering a collective experience of network and shared exercise.

11.Four Pilgrimage and Sacred Sites

Pilgrimage holds a massive region in Buddhism, with practitioners touring to sacred internet websites related to the life of the Buddha or one-of-a-kind reputable

Buddhist figures. Pilgrimage gives an possibility to deepen one's connection to the spiritual direction, get keep of advantages, and domesticate devotion.

Pilgrimage internet websites can encompass the birthplace of the Buddha in Lumbini, the net site online of his enlightenment in Bodh Gaya, and the location of his first sermon in Sarnath. Other brilliant pilgrimage locations encompass the historical metropolis of Varanasi, the holy mountain of Kailash, and the Buddhist pilgrimage circuit in Tibet.

Pilgrimage isn't always constrained to bodily tour but can also be undertaken in a metaphorical feel, symbolizing the inward journey closer to self-transformation and enlightenment. Itrepresents the strength of will to religious growth, the deepening of 1's religion, and the exploration of sacred teachings and locations.

eleven.5 Engaging in Generosity and Service

Generosity, called dana in Buddhism, is a important exercising that cultivates selflessness, compassion, and the popularity of interdependence. Practitioners interact in acts of generosity through supplying donations, helping monastic agencies, and attractive in acts of service to others.

Through acts of generosity, humans domesticate a sense of detachment from cloth possessions and boom a deep data of the interconnectedness of all beings. Generosity fosters traits which encompass compassion, kindness, and the popularity of the inherent nicely properly really worth and dignity of anybody.

www.ingramcontent.com/pod-product-compliance
Lightning Source LLC
Chambersburg PA
CBHW071440080526
44587CB00014B/1924